AF380641

NEDA SAEEDI

WHISPERS

PODERE TRAFONTI
MOUSSE PUBLISHING

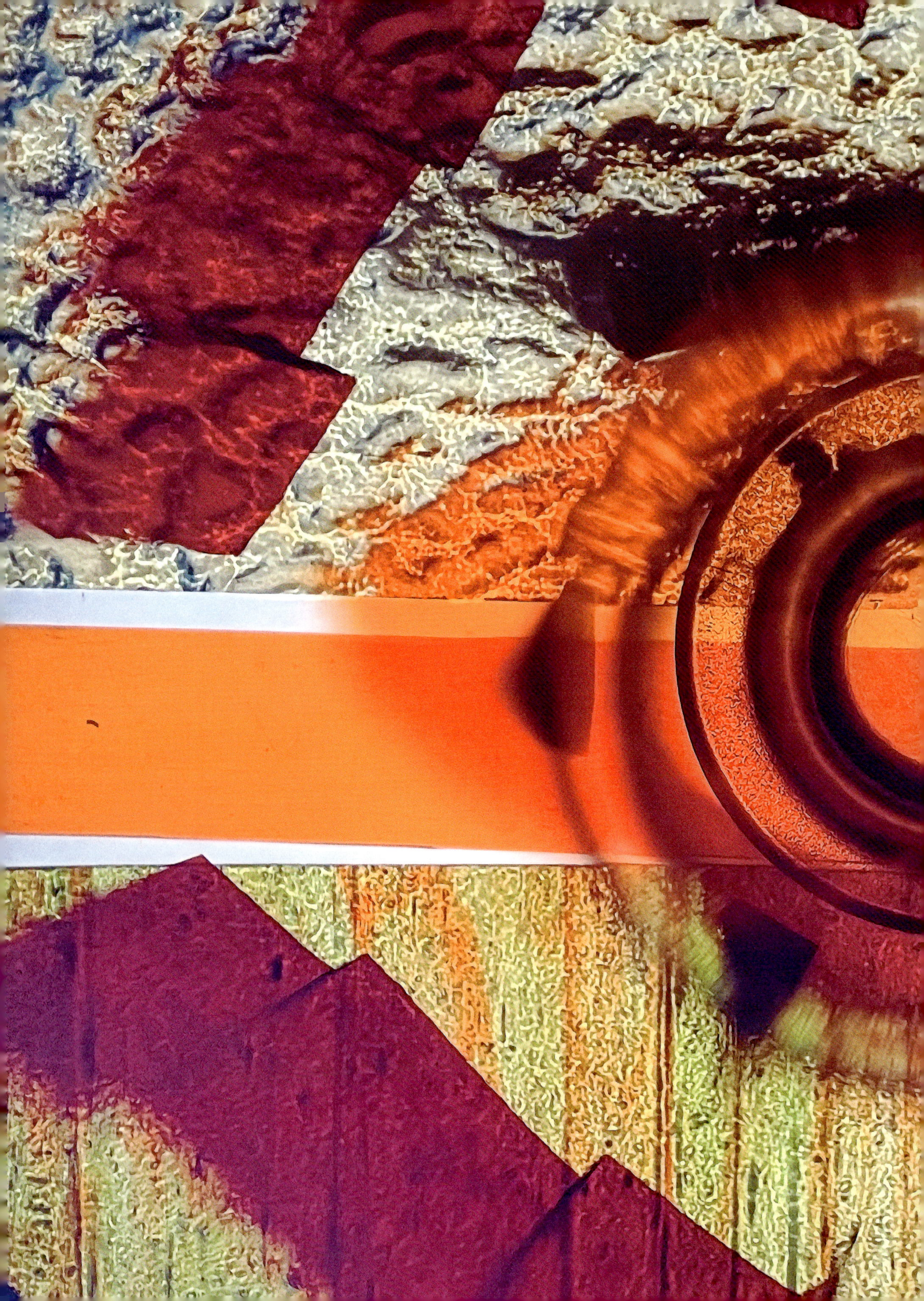

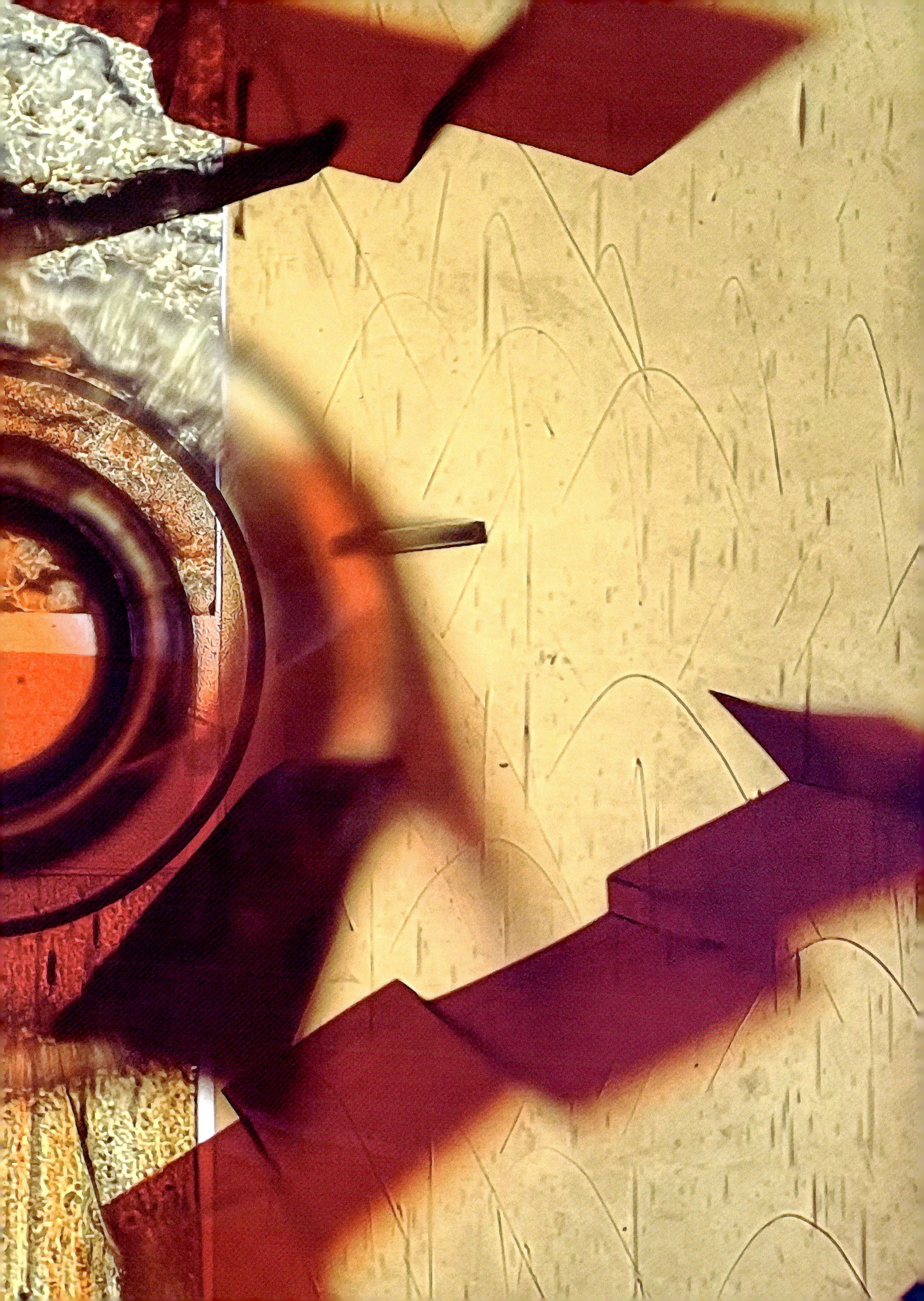

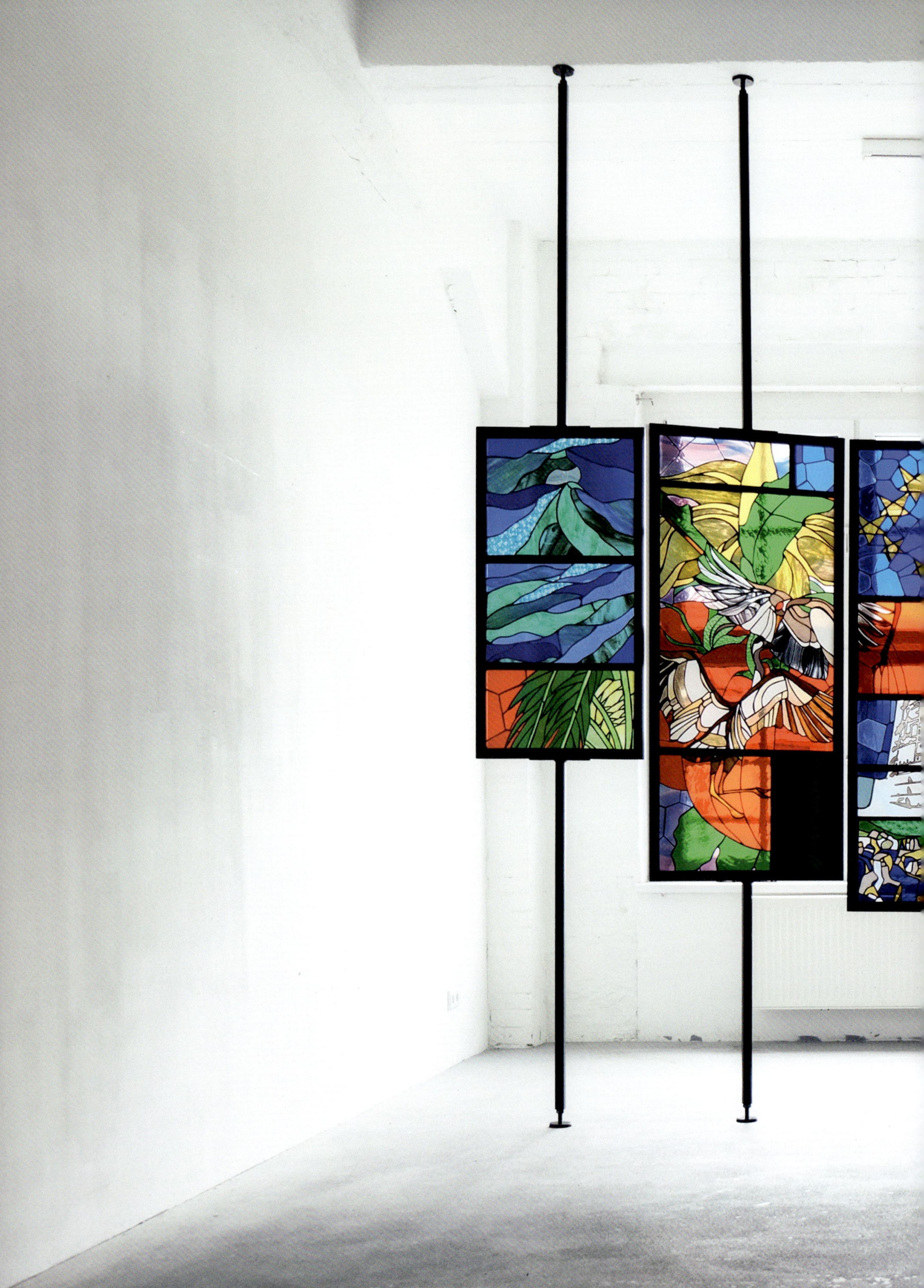

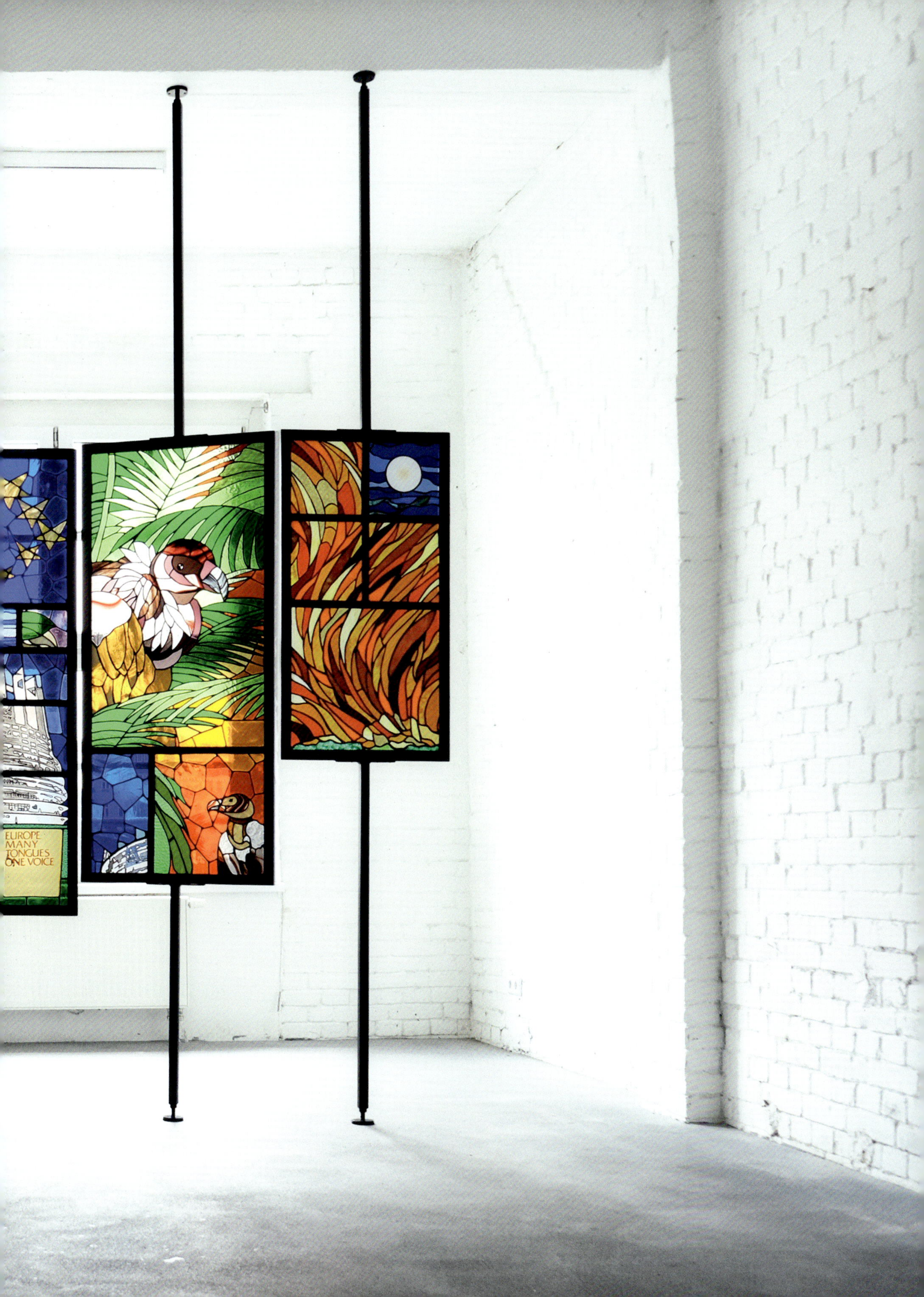
EUROPE
MANY
TONGUES
ONE VOICE

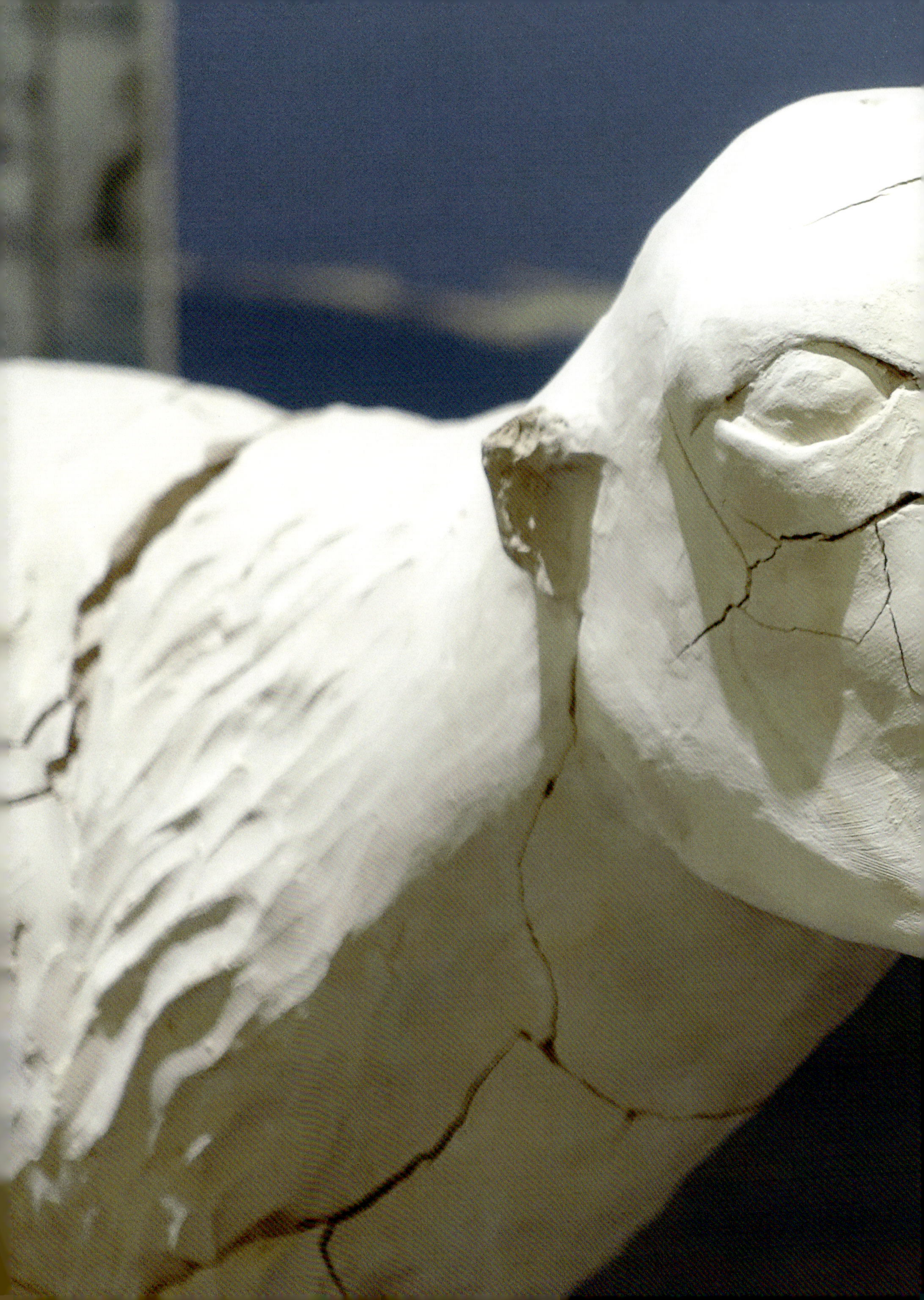

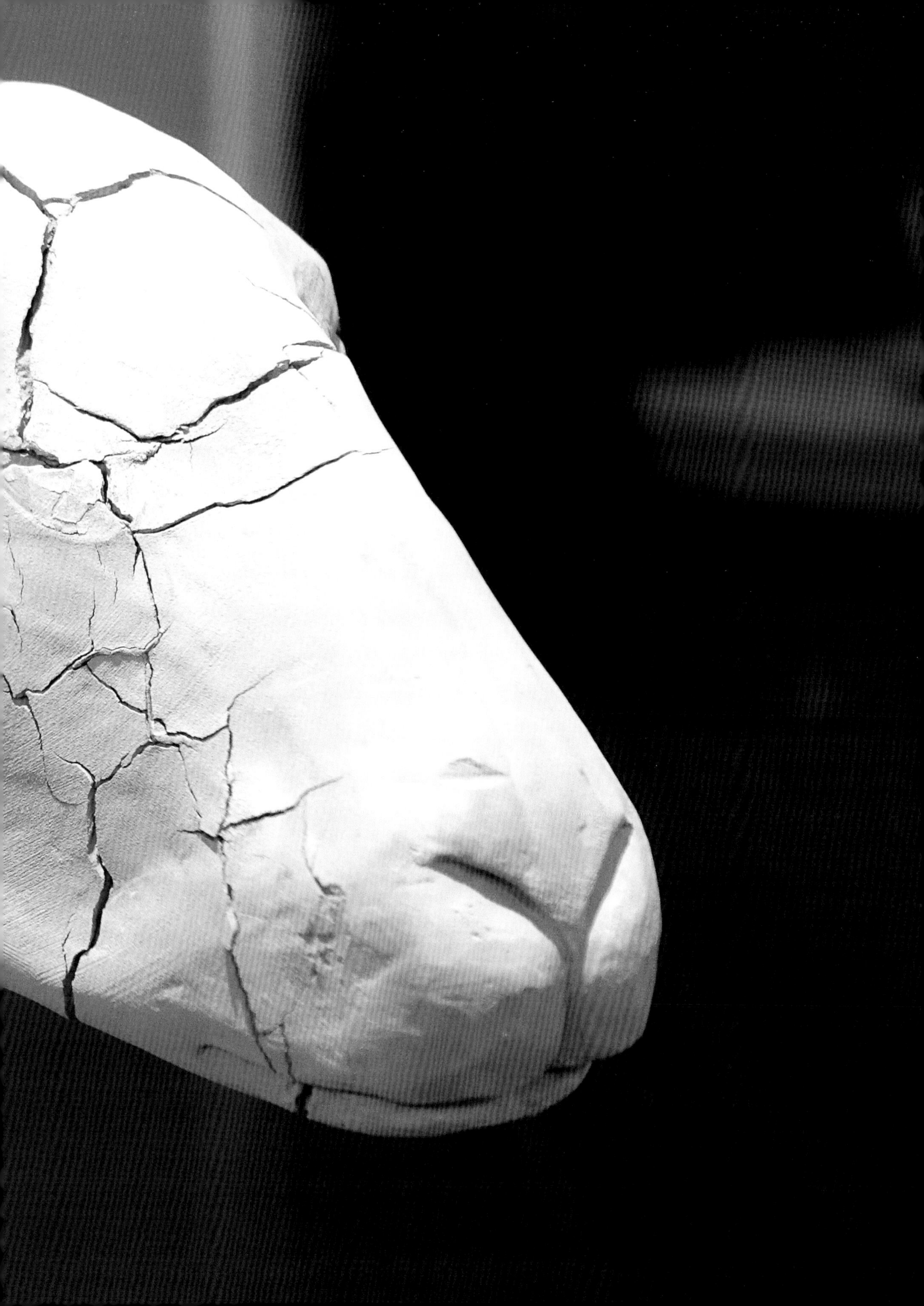

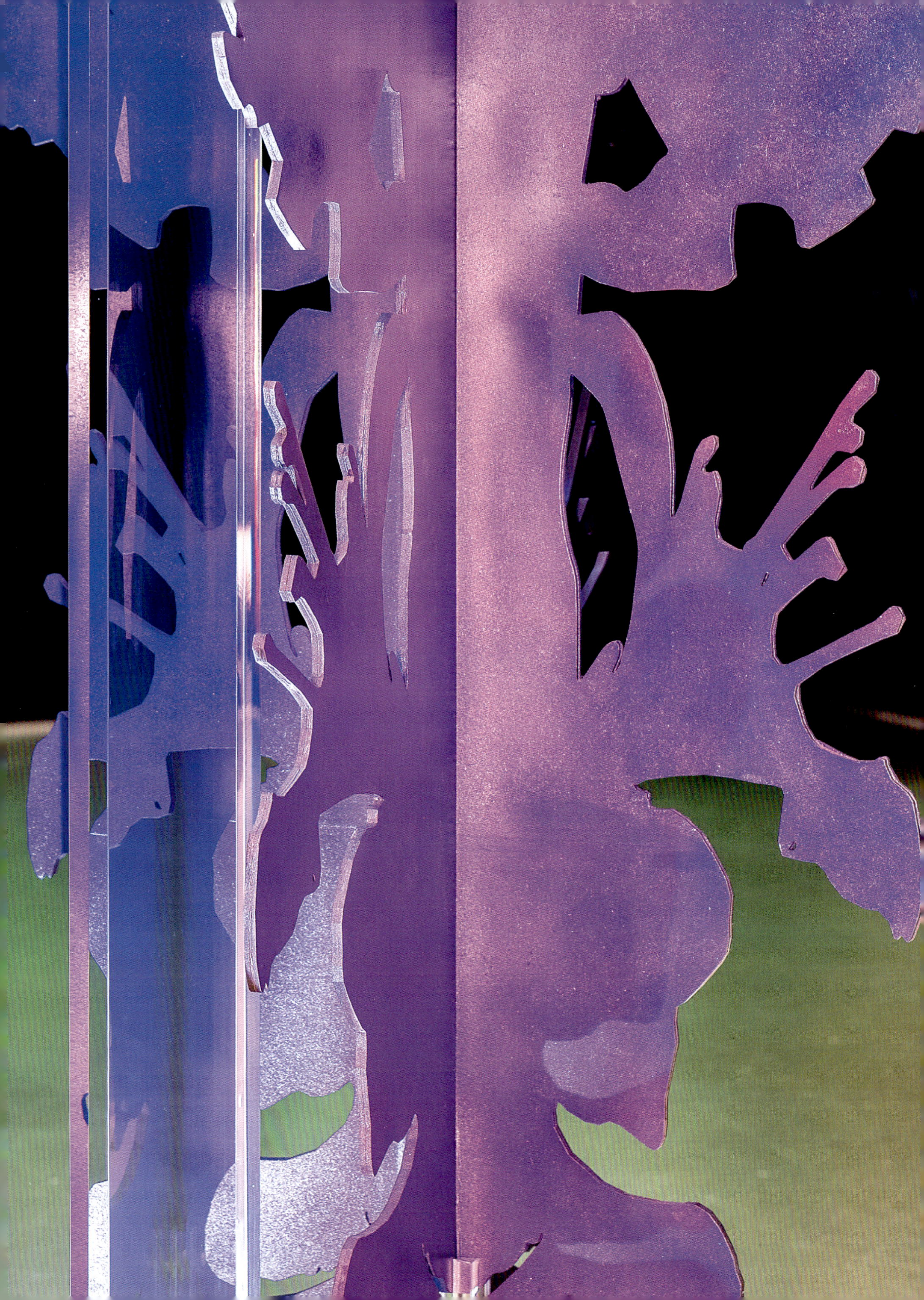

TABLE OF CONTENTS

15–20

23–27

65–80

122–124

WALKING AROUND A GARDEN AND TELLING EACH OTHER STORIES

*Neda Saeedi; on Silent Witnesses
and the Agency of Matter*

Yasmin Afschar

1816 went down in history as the 'year without a summer'. During an eruption in April 1815, the volcano of Mount Tambora, in present-day Indonesia, spewed unimaginable amounts of ash and dust into the atmosphere, which enveloped the Earth like a veil and caused global temperatures to cool. It is said to have snowed in southern Italy in June, resulting in crop failures and food shortages. In that very year without a summer, Faustina Pecci Landucci, an aristocrat in Montefollonico in Tuscany, commissioned the construction of a garden for her house to help the farmers and labourers who worked for her through the cropless year. The garden was classically divided into a formalised part according to Italian tradition, a 'wild' part, and a vegetable and hanging garden with views over the rolling Tuscan hills. Neda Saeedi tells me the story of the Villa Marselli garden on one of the first evenings I visit her during her residency at Podere Trafonti. The garden is a thirty-minute walk from the patio above the main house where we sit—its view equally sublime.

Neda is interested in gardens as a crystallisation point for the interrelationships between culture, nature and power. Let's take our example from Montefollonico: the Italian garden, strictly organised and staged by human hands, 'needs' the wild counterpart to demonstrate the superiority of culture over nature. Likewise, the aristocrat confronted the seemingly uncontrollable power of nature—manifested in the volcanic eruption and the darkened sky—by building a garden, a piece of controlled nature. By doing so, she not only ensured peace in the community but also the productivity and loyalty of the peasants in the years that followed, thus fuelling a capitalist system of ever-increasing profits.

According to Neda, gardens are based on activities of collecting, defining, evaluating, and classifying—activities that correspond to the fundamental principles of colonialism.[1] As Neda and I will discuss later, the history of gardens has almost always been linked to capitalism, class and segregation—and their foothills in the sphere of religion. The ancient Persian word for garden is 'pari-daizi', which means 'enclosure' or 'walled'. The term entered European languages via Ancient Greek and Latin as 'paradise', underlying how gardens have always served as powerful metaphors, symbolising the divine *and* representing imperialistic power.

1   See Ana Teixeira Pinto in conversation with Neda Saeedi, in Neda Saeedi, *Only Birds Who Fly the Highest Can Shatter the Windows* (Florence: Villa Romana, 2022) p. 35.

Neda shares yet another story with me, one of many that follow. This one is the starting point for her work *Two Shades of Green* (2021): the Conocarpus is an evergreen tree that grows throughout West Africa from Senegal to Angola, in the Caribbean, on the coasts of Central and South America and in Florida. It is said to have been brought from Florida to Dubai in the 1970s to satisfy the search for greenery for the residential areas of a metal factory. Soon, the invasive, water-intensive and even harmful plants had spread throughout the Arab Emirates. At the beginning of the 2000s, Conocarpus reached southern Iran. It is said to have appeared around a factory in the industrial zone of Bandar Abbas which sourced its products in Dubai. Today, the shrubby tree characterises the cityscape of several industrial locations in the area. Much greener than the sparse native vegetation and not dependent on the seasons, it serves the image of Western cities and their generous plantings. This desire for a 'better shade of green', i.e. a shade of green connoted with the West, literally grew into a health problem. In the Indian state of Gujarat, Conocarpus was banned last year due to allergic reactions, respiratory diseases and the danger it poses to native plants. The talk was about a *green desert*.

The invasive mangrove tree in *Two Shades of Green*, a work that Neda displayed in Tehran at the Pejman Foundation and in Baden-Baden at the Staatliche Kunsthalle, is representative of the modes of displacement that go hand in hand with laying a garden. Neda here dismantles the promises of the garden as a romantic retreat and place of recreative rapture and instead demonstrates its inherently exclusionary logic of supremacy and fencing-off, in this case, the 'wild', and 'inferior' native plants. She subjects native plants to a process known as 'decellularisation'—a biomedical procedure in which the cells of living beings are emptied so that only the dead shell texture remains. She then colours these in a brilliant 'artificial' green. Presented in snow globes, they provoke associations with museum displays and the comparative presentation with which 'finds' from the colonial era are often presented in the Global North. Speaking to notions of migration and the governance of nature, the septically isolated objects seem ready to be channelled through the global history of gardening, just as the subjugation and domination of nature aims to control and ultimately exclude the 'other'.

It seems reasonable to me to suggest that Neda is engaged in a form of *future archaeology*.

The blending, layering and intertwining of time and place is a key characteristic of Persian miniature painting. Within a single picture, scenes from various moments in time are combined and arranged on the basis of their relevance to the subject rather than their chronological order. For instance, just because we see a scene with stars, it doesn't automatically imply that the story is set at night. Likewise, the arrangement of architecture, people, flora and fauna is symbolic in nature. Both objects and beings have the same weight—they share an equal legibility. Incidentally, the term 'miniature' is a colonial creation, a collective term for figurative paintings created in present-day Iran, Turkey and Central and South Asia. Due to the influence of imperialist powers and the changing forms of governance, numerous illustrated manuscripts ended up in private collections and museums across Europe. Many of these manuscripts were then disassembled to facilitate their sale and exhibition, however, making them inaccessible to those whose stories they depicted. Picture this: in 1994, the Museum of Contemporary Art in Tehran traded a de Kooning painting (of a naked woman) to get back part of a sixteenth-century Shahnameh manuscript—secretly at Vienna Airport. This act took place after decades of extractivist patronage, which also led to the decline of the craft itself in many regions. Neda and I discuss the non-linear structure and, at the same time, the meticulousness of the paintings. Their aim is to overwhelm the senses, shifting away from a human perspective and the pursuit of naturalism that characterised Western art history. Instead, they claim to offer nothing less than a glimpse through and into the eyes of God.

Gardens, as expected, play a significant role in the illuminated manuscripts tradition. They depict paradise, where nature serves as a spiritual link to divine creation, emphasising a spiritual and humble view of the natural world, in contrast to the Western idea of man's dominance over nature.

In her exploration of the concept of paradise as an 'enclosed', 'walled' garden, Neda directed her attention to these physical boundaries as they are represented in miniature painting. She meticulously analysed illustrations, isolating the architectural elements surrounding depictions of gardens, specifically walls and fractions that surround or uncover a view into a garden. Reducing them to their geometric outlines, Neda collected them in an unpublished plan, resembling the blueprint for a timeless and placeless fortress. It contains the outlines of around sixty such architectural typologies. From this compendium of patterns, Neda then produced metal wall objects by enlarging fragments from the plan, effectively creating railings. This process highlights the 'fencing off' characteristic of the garden.

Whispers Across Horizons is a site-specific installation created by Neda on the back wall of the main house in Trafonti in early 2024. The installation originates from a fraction of a miniature painting and brings to life the 'excluded' garden by incorporating the natural surroundings of Trafonti, such as olive trees, cypresses, fields, a vegetable garden and bushes. The original geometric drawing is transformed into a significant structural element through enlargement. Neda enhances the window recesses of the windowless wall with mirror works, creating a fictional view that reflects the surrounding environment and the observer through its kaleidoscopic geometry. Drawing from Islamic ornamentation and sacred geometry, Neda's mirror compositions feature crystalline sun, star and plant shapes reminiscent of both mandalas and scientific illustrations. Different coloured mirrors are used to signify different times of day: night, sunrise and sunset, presenting a rhythmic portrayal of a day and the interconnectedness of past, present and future, as well as connecting the physical spaces before and behind us. The fragmented mirrors in Persian mirror-tile work symbolise the idea of unity in multiplicity, echoing the Persian philosophical notion of the 'wholeness of space'. Mirror-flooded spaces overcome optical and physical boundaries to illustrate the interconnectedness of all things. In Neda's case, they serve as an artistic exploration of the connections between nature and humans, as echoed in the work's subtitle, 'A Symphony of Persian Reverie in Nature's Embrace'. In the mirror fragments, we only ever see ourselves in parts—and therefore always as part of the nature that surrounds us. More-than-human and human life forms a shimmering ornament that constantly changes depending on the season, the weather or one's position. In Sufi philosophy, mirrors are also a metaphor for inner contemplation and self-awareness, here reminding us of nature's own ability to reflect our gaze back at us.

Someone once told me that exile is the ability to *look at things in layers*. Isn't that exactly what Persian illuminated manuscripts do? Just like Neda's contemporary interpretations.

Let's stay with mirrors for a moment and the idea that they can have agency as material, as part of a work of art, as well as in the way they reflect the world. A central statement by the theorist Jane Bennett is that *matter is active*; she considers it to be vital: "By 'vitality' I mean the capacity of things—edibles, commodities, storms, metals—not only to impede or block the will and designs of humans, but also to act as quasi-agents or forces with trajectories, propensities or tendencies of their own."[2] Bennett speaks of the power of things, of the emancipation of the non-human, and argues from the standpoint of political-ecology. Listening to things—understanding material as an agent of social and political life—as material witnesses with their own power of expression and evidence can also be a strategy against the politics of silencing, as Gayatri Chakravorty Spivak describes them in *Can the Subaltern Speak?* in relation to racial capitalism based on exclusion.

Every object and material Neda uses in her work tells its own story. Having studied classical sculpture in Tehran, she knows her material well and observes it closely. It should possess capabilities that extend beyond the formal; its functionality ought to be genuinely impactful rather than merely illustrative. Handmade mirror tiles, artificial 3D-prints next to decellularised plants in snow domes, a sugary object that recalls the forced settlement of nomadic tribes or artificially produced crystals that you must first destroy in order to determine their authenticity! The materials Neda uses have their own biography, their own reality and memory. Sugar, for example, played a significant role in the early days of globalisation, while the act of compressing and flattening for the herbarium represents the violence inherent in collecting and souvenirs. I am reminded of how the sociologist Avery Gordon talks about *following* 'the ghosts': the excluded narratives and unmapped chapters of world history, which manifest themselves not least in objects and matter, she argues, to make "a contact that changes you and refashions the social relations in which you are located,"[3] as the ghost harbours transformative potential. Something or someone who has been silenced returns to reality in a reckoning to "settle accounts."

2 Jane Bennett, *Vibrant Matter: A Political Ecology of Things* (Durham, NC: Duke University Press, 2010), p. viii.
3 Avery F. Gordon, *Ghostly Matters: Haunting and the Sociological Imagination* (Minneapolis: University of Minnesota Press, 2008), p. 22, 183.

The conceptual and physical proximity that Neda maintains to the material and its agency was also decisive in the conception of this book. The pictures are predominantly close-ups and details. We have abandoned reflecting on spatial perception, otherwise essential for the trained sculptor, in favour of 'visual touches'. We scroll along structures, light, colours, surfaces and membranes, which seem reciprocal and to be affecting each other. The material is superimposed, just as time and place are layered in Persian painting. Neda tells me that only the processing of the material leads from one idea to the other, not the reading and research, which are also central to her practice. The semi-transparent pages in the book allow views that symbolise the conversation that the materials and images in Neda's work have with each other and with us. Being inside and outside, the question of perspective (doesn't the striving for an overview merely serve the promises of hegemonic supremacist thinking?) culminates in an examination of the politics of the view and gaze.

In Persian, Neda means 'voice' or 'divine message'. Without a doubt, Neda is a storyteller. Her installations not only work by overlaying stories, places and times, but they are also a little bit like the stained-glass windows found in churches that are considered the 'Bible for the poor'. Neda's works also incorporate a choreography of movements. Their narratives are silent yet polyphonic and multi-layered, the objects and materials serve as protagonists, each with its own language. Experiencing Neda Saeedi's work can be like walking around a garden and telling each other stories. This idea of 'returning to neverland', a concept that also lends its name to an artist book featuring a conversation between Neda and Homayoun Sirizi, can provide a framework for looking at her installations in general as well as for leafing through this book.

TO SEE THROUGH AND TO LOOK BEHIND

On the Politics of Portals in the Work of Neda Saeedi

Carina Bukuts

A window for seeing
A window for hearing
A window like a well
that ends deep in the heart of the Earth
and opens out into this expanse of recurring blue kindness
A window that overfills the tiny hands of loneliness
with its nightly gift: the perfume of generous stars
And from there one could invite the sun to the geraniums in exile
One window is enough for me

Forough Farrokhzad[1]

Arguably, there are very few situations in public life in which we are not being directed. Most of our behaviour in public space follows implemented protocols that we follow for the sake of efficiency. Ideally, artworks allow us to put all this aside for a moment. Nobody tells you how long you should stand in front of a painting, or at which angle a sculpture should be looked at, and there is no time limit on the engagement. Rather than imposing, artworks are nothing but mere invitations.

Throughout her practice, artist Neda Saeedi has taken different approaches to formulating such invitations, but what unites them all is the artist's interest in states of transformation. Following long periods of research, she looks at moments in time—either lifted from histories that are no longer being told or conditions within our present—in which conversion has occurred *or* is on its way. For the 2018 edition of the Luleå Biennial, Saaedi turned her eye towards the history of her homeland, Iran. Two years prior to this exhibition, she visited Shushtar-e Nou (Engl. Shushtar New Town), a town established in the 1970s close to the ancient city of Shushtar, best known for its historic hydraulic system, which can be traced back to Darius the Great in the fifth century BCE. Whoever embarks on the journey of visiting Shushtar will be awarded with spectacular cliffs and cascades, canals and qanats,[2] channelling the waters of the Karun River for irrigation and power generation. In contrast, Shushtar-e Nou follows a grid-like pattern with the promise of ensuring efficient navigation. Residential areas are meticulously organised into compact, rectangular blocks, which are symmetrically arranged around a central axis. All of these characteristics are indicative of an approach

---

1   From 'Window', trans. Elizabeth T. Gray Jr, *The Paris Review* 223, Summer 2020.
2   Qanats are ancient underground water channels originating in Persia, designed
    to transport water from aquifers to the surface for irrigation and drinking.
    They consist of a series of vertical shafts connected by a gently sloping tunnel,
    which uses gravity to move water efficiently while minimising evaporation.

to urban design and planning that favours cohesiveness—and there-by the politics of assimilation and uniformity—over multiplicity. In an interview with the curator Asrin Haidari, Saeedi described how she was interested in the city because, despite the international recognition the architecture received,[3] she had always considered it "highly controlled and suffocating".[4] More than a subjective impression, it seems as if the artist had a sixth sense concerning the undermining politics of this development project, which have been buried over the past fifty years since its inauguration. By digging deeper—as per the modus operandi of Saeedi's research-based practice—she discovered that the history of Shushtar-e Nou is essentially one of displacement: with the aim of modernising the country and exercising greater control over the population, the Iranian government under the rule of Reza Shah Pahlavi and his son Moham-mad Reza Shah pursued an aggressive sedentarisation policy in the late 1960s, known as the White Revolution. The creation of Shushtar-e Nou, which saw the containment of the Bachtiaris tribe, was part of this larger strategy to settle nomads in permanent housing, thereby disrupting their traditional migratory patterns and ways of life. In an attempt to kill two birds with one stone, the historical town of Shushtar was set to house an imported sugar cane farm and a corresponding refinery where sugar could be produced for the USA, who had lost their main sugar supplier with the country's imposed embargo against Cuba in 1958. As a result, the population of the Bachtiaris tribe as well as many more nomads from the region were supposed to staff the newly established sugar factories and live in Shushtar-e Nou.

In *Garden of Eden Moving; A Petrified Tribe* (2018), first shown at the Luleå Konsthall, Saeedi gives visual form to this violent history by means of consolidation. The first gesture confronting visitors is a massive wall on which moving images are projected of a flock of sheep, archival footage from the Bachtiaris tribe with their herd. A little square hole within the structure allows a glimpse through to the other side, and, when moving around the installation, it becomes evident that the design of the wall is intended to recall a water dam, with the opening in the wall resembling those through which water would flow into reservoirs. Instead of fluids, however, transparent lollipops—as if frozen in time—pour out onto the floor of the gallery space. In front of this dam of sweetness stands a sheep cast from sugar. While the animal serves as a symbol of the Bachtiaris

3   Shushtar-e Nou was awarded the Aga Khan Award for Architecture, which it won in the 1984–1986 cycle. Additionally, Shushtar-e Nou was included in the travelling exhibition *At the End of the Century: One Hundred Years of Architecture*, which toured several venues including the Museum of Contemporary Art, Los Angeles (MOCA), the Museum of Contemporary Art, Tokyo and Museum Ludwig, Cologne.
4   In *Lulu Journal 5* (January 2019), https://www.luleabiennial.se/en/journalen/nr-5/neda-saeedi (accessed 25 July 2024).

tribe's reliance on livestock, which provided sustenance, milk as well as wool and leather for clothing, it's the sculpture's hollowness and delicate material that speaks to the vulnerability of these ancestral ways of life.

Elsewhere in the exhibition space, a series of sculptures of upturned carcasses reminds us that where there is sweetness, bitterness is never far away—as the colonial history of sugar can attest to. Additionally, as Saeedi found out, over the course of the past decades, the sugar mill in Shushtar has been leaking hazardous waste, causing the once significant wetland to turn into a wasteland. In this respect, it seems almost paradoxical that in the financial world the ease with which an asset or security can be converted into cash is referred to as 'liquidity', when it's the very capitalist rush for money that leads an entire ecosystem to dry out. While the Iranian Revolution (1978–79) shows how little the people agreed with the Shah's autocratic ruling, the stories and politics that Saeedi unearths are far from known among a wider public, which made the presentation of these works at the Dastan Basement (2019), in her hometown of Tehran, even more important.

While the artist urges us to examine these historical blind spots, I would argue that her sculptures equally encourage us to reimagine other kinds of acts of transformation. In *Garden of Eden Moving; A Petrified Tribe*, the devil lies in the details: it's the hole in the dam that can also be understood as a portal of possibilities. If Saeedi uses the dam to create an analogy between the containment of water and the containment of people, it seems that the hole alludes to the strength and resilience of water, which finds ways to overcome any obstacle, no matter how great.

The idea of openings within structures also looms large in other works by the artist. For many years, she has been studying the history and architecture of windows—particularly those featured in spiritual places. In a conversation with Saeedi, we spoke about how organised religions might be the best developers, as their buildings have consistently showcased the finest materials available during their respective eras despite the implied costs.[5] Over the past four years, Saeedi's research brought her for a substantial amount of time to Italy—whether for her residency with Podere Trafonti in the Siena region in 2023 or her stay with Villa Romana in Florence in 2022. With an estimated 65,000 churches across the country, it appears only natural that the buildings leave an impact on you.

5   In her 2008 drawing *Landscape with Still Life*, the Brazilian artist Marie Thereza Alves stated that "the first gold taken from Mexico after its conquest was used to decorate the church of Santa Maria Maggiore in Rome", drawing attention to the colonial past of the materials used in Christian churches throughout Italy.

Across past and recent art history, there are many artists who come to mind who have been invited to design a church window: think of Gerhard Richter's 11,300 coloured squares in the Cathedral of Cologne, the stained glass painted in blue by Marc Chagall for the Fraumünster Church in Zurich or the Rosary Chapel in Vence, where Henri Matisse's composition of yellow, green and blue floods the entire space. Looking at the names of the artists whose work was considered good enough to commune with the 'almighty', it is shocking—yet given the institution's record of patriarchal oppression, hardly surprising—that none of them are women.

In many ways Saeedi's *Only Birds Who Fly the Highest Can Shatter the Windows* (2022) is a monument to all those who have been—and continue to be—excluded from predominant systems of control. The altarpiece, consisting of a series of five windows of stained glass mounted on metal poles, depicts the golden stars from the European Union flag hovering like a crown of thorns above the circular building of the European Parliament in Strasbourg, evoking Pieter Bruegel the Elders's *Tower of Babel* (1563). Below a text reads "Europe, many tongues, one voice," while the other panels feature colourful migratory birds on the one side and curious-looking vultures on the other. As architectural elements that allow the entry of light, windows suggest openness. In her installation, Saeedi provides another reading, highlighting the ways in which windows also shield the inside from external influences, thus creating a barrier between what belongs and what does not. Through blending this inviting gesture with a defensive one, she finds an adequate metaphor for a European migration policy which, while advertising multiplicity, in reality often places those seeking to be included in its Tower of Babel on the other side of the window.[6]

Not only do birds feature prominently again in *In the Depth of the Night, Sky Sees the Sun* (2023), commissioned for the 4th Autostrada Biennale, but the work is also a continuation of Saeedi's exploration of the potential of glass as material. The massive sculpture spans a diameter of 420 cm and is influenced by the artist's research on Fresnel lenses that were initially created for lighthouses. Composed of concentric rings that step up in height and scale, the lens creates a soft-edged beam and—more importantly—allows for light to travel over great distances. Showing six blackbirds in front of a colourful landscape some viewers might mistake this work as merely a highly aesthetical play of lights and colours in

---

6   Genesis 11:1–9 contains the biblical account of the Tower of Babel, which represents human arrogance and ambition. Speaking the same language, humanity attempted to construct a tower that would reach the skies after the Great Flood. According to the Bible, God stopped the building by dispersing them around the planet and mumbling their language. Allegedly, the story illustrates the genesis of several languages.

the public space of Prizren's League Square. However, those who take a
closer look will quickly understand that for Saeedi, imagery and materials are never neutral but always signifiers of political circumstances.
The sculpture takes inspiration from the etymology of the word 'Kosovo'
(or 'field of blackbirds' in English) and is again a comment on migration.
Unlike the Bachtiaris tribe, whose life was defined by constant movement,
blackbirds have a unique sense of residence and only migrate in times
of hardship. While Saeedi employs glass in *Only Birds Who Fly the Highest
Can Shatter the Windows* to touch upon the concept of the glass ceiling
for those deemed alien, the use of the Fresnel lenses in *In the Depth of
the Night, Sky Sees the Sun* hints at methods of overcoming vast distances
and the respective obstacles. As with other works by the artist, it's the
site-specific context that adds another layer to this reading. During the
Biennial, the sculpture occupied the vacant space in a rectangular frame
that once hosted the anti-fascist monument *Heronjte e popullit–Agimi i Liris*
('The Heroes of the People—the Dawn of Freedom') honouring partisans
who fought during World War II. While the statues initially erected there
were made of bronze, their removal demonstrates how little a material
that might convey solidity and permanence can actually withstand in
lack of political will. In turn, Saeedi's translucent glass piece at once highlights such empty promises and acts as a portal, prompting us to look
back on our past as well as encouraging us to never stop beyond it.

I was studying the role of light in sculpture-making, and how it is actually a very crucial element, although it's not the centre of attention when we talk about classical sculpture.

But any sculptor thinks about the light:
the source of light, the direction of light,
and so on and so forth.

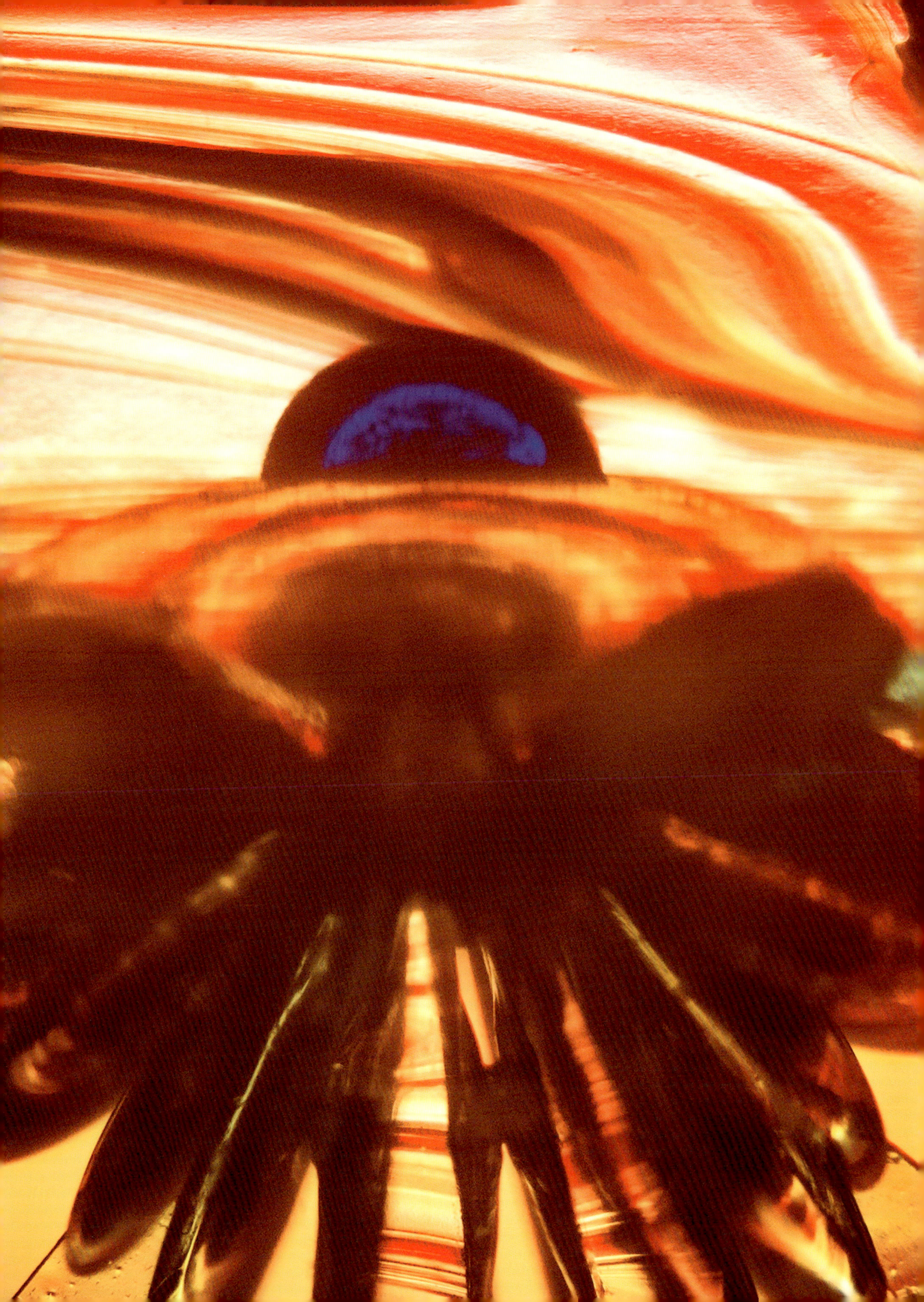

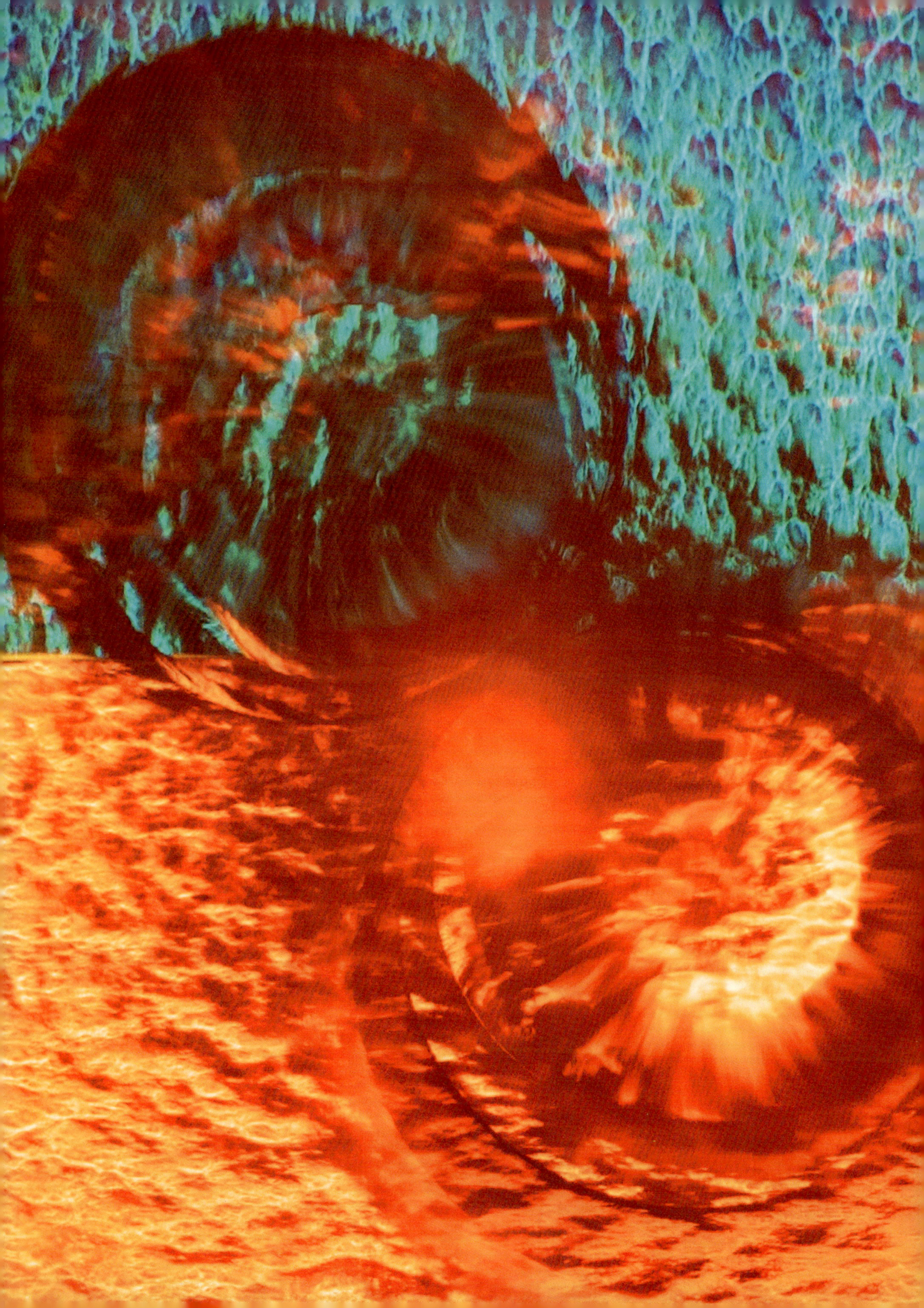

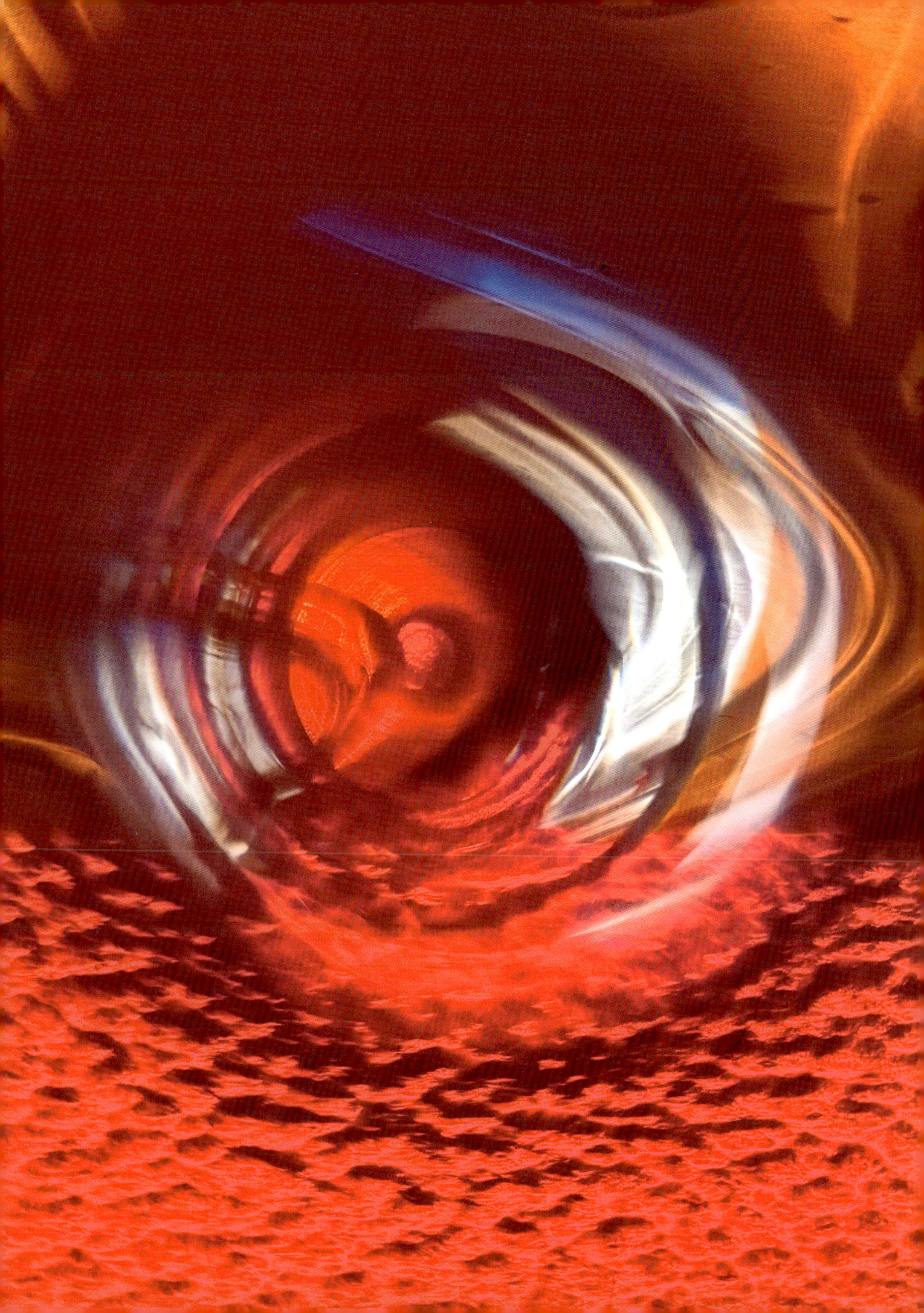

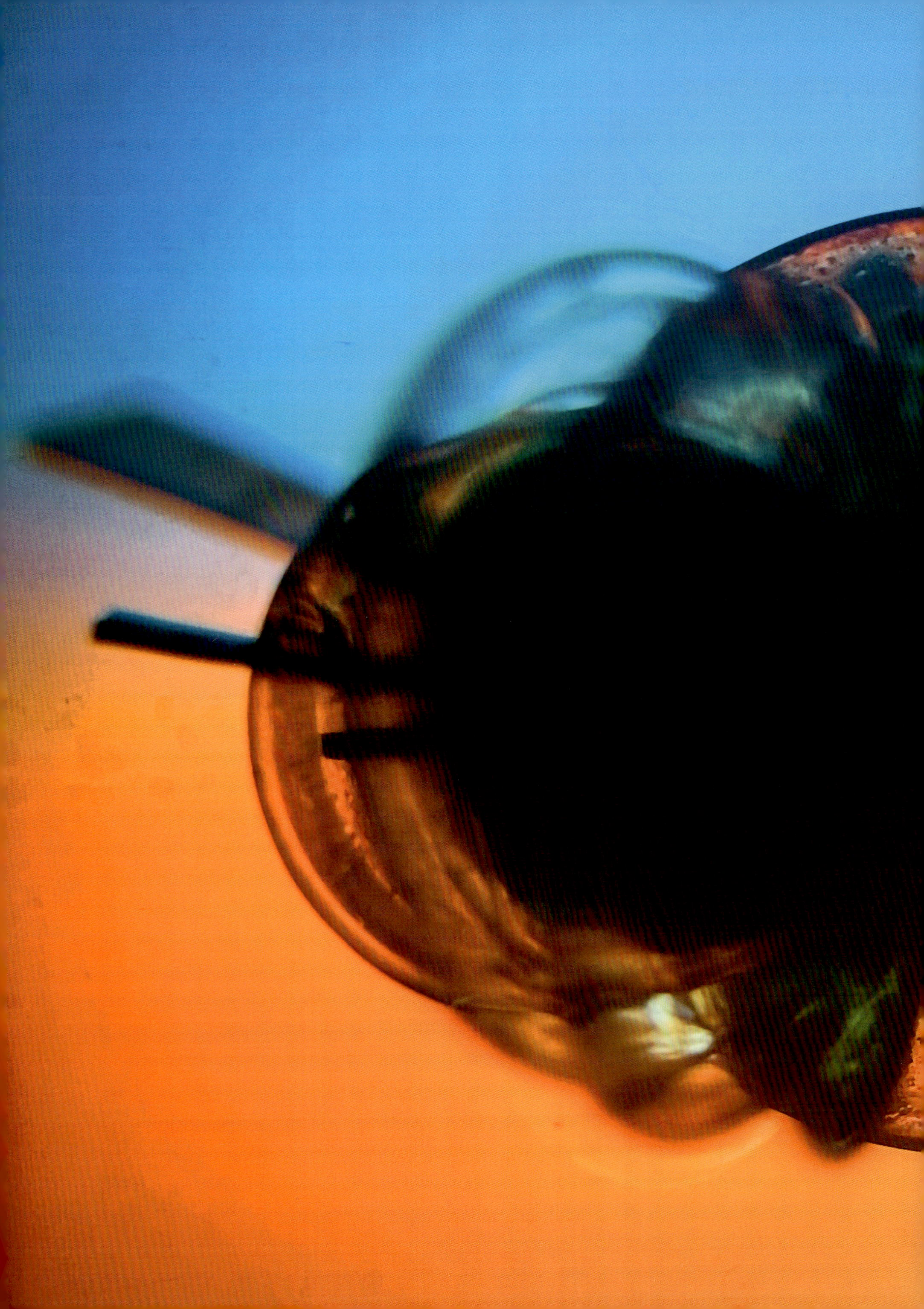

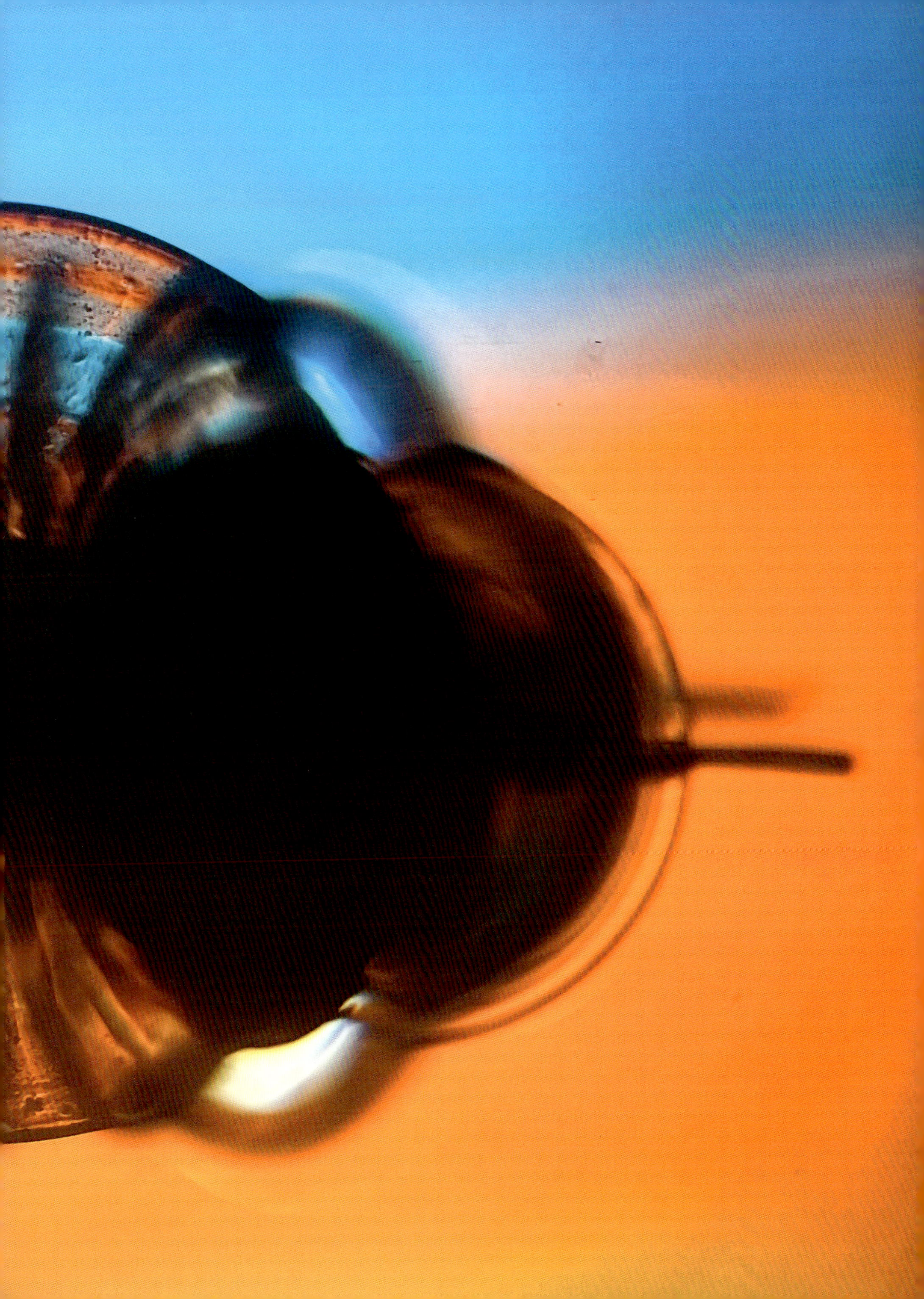

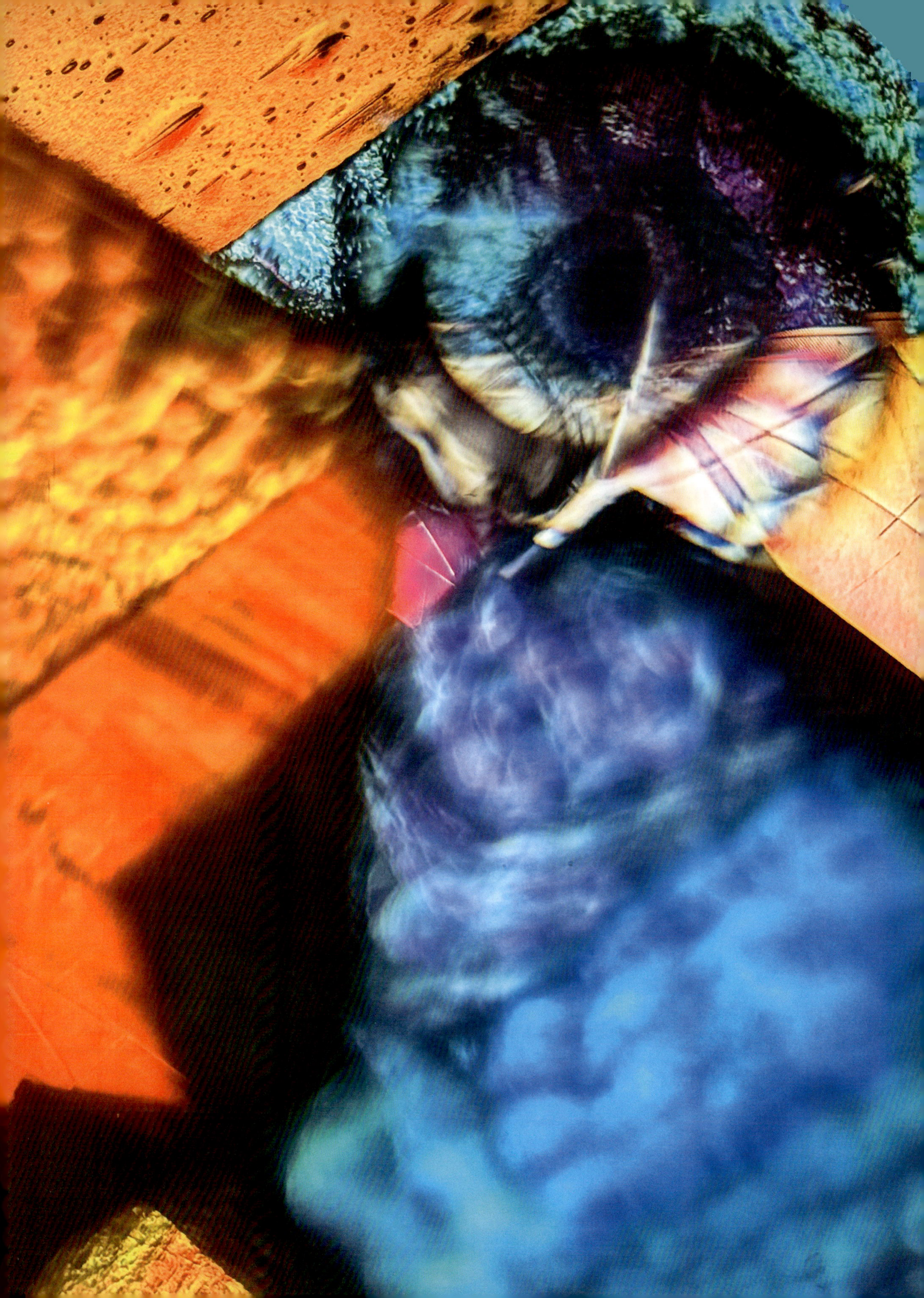

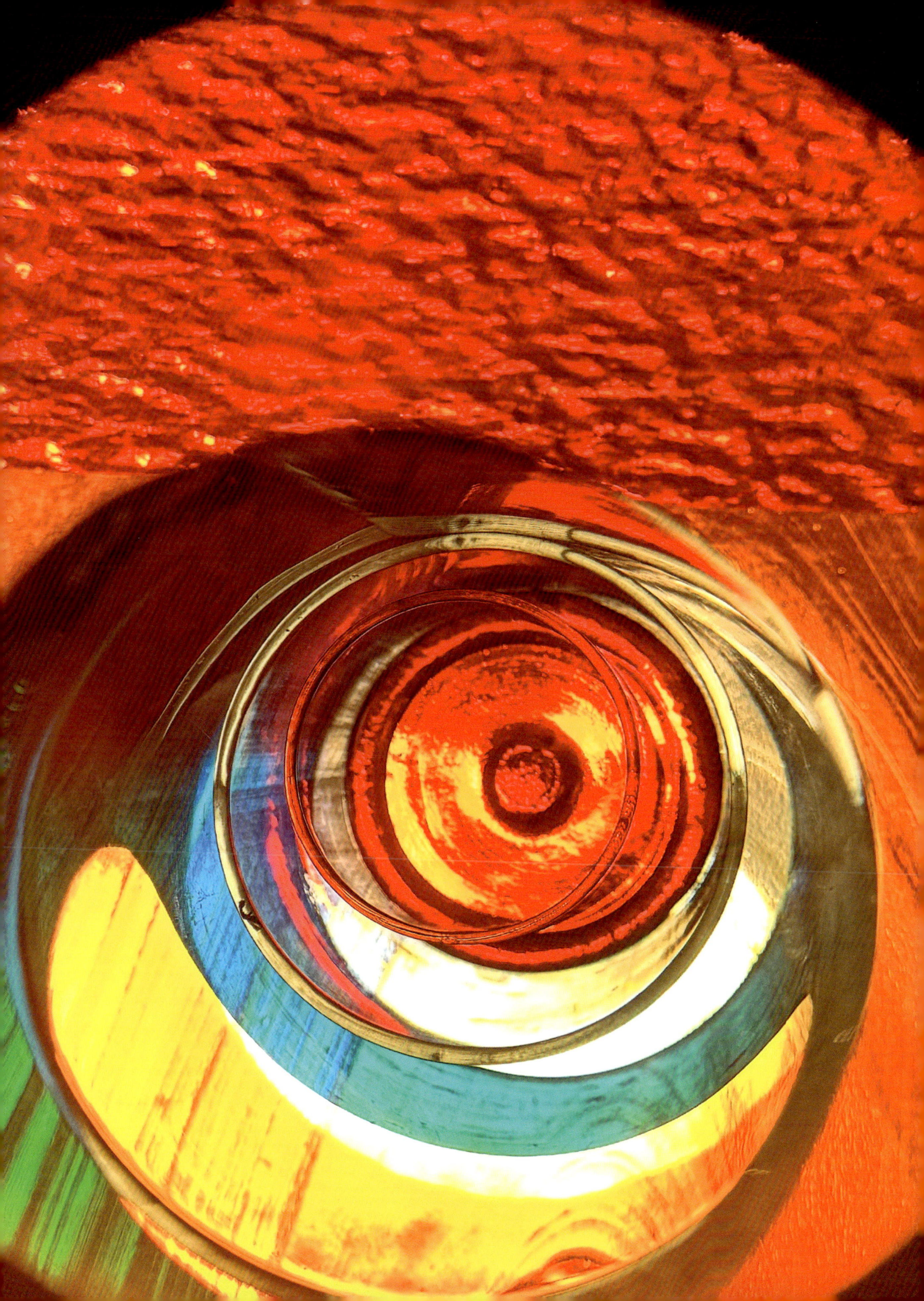

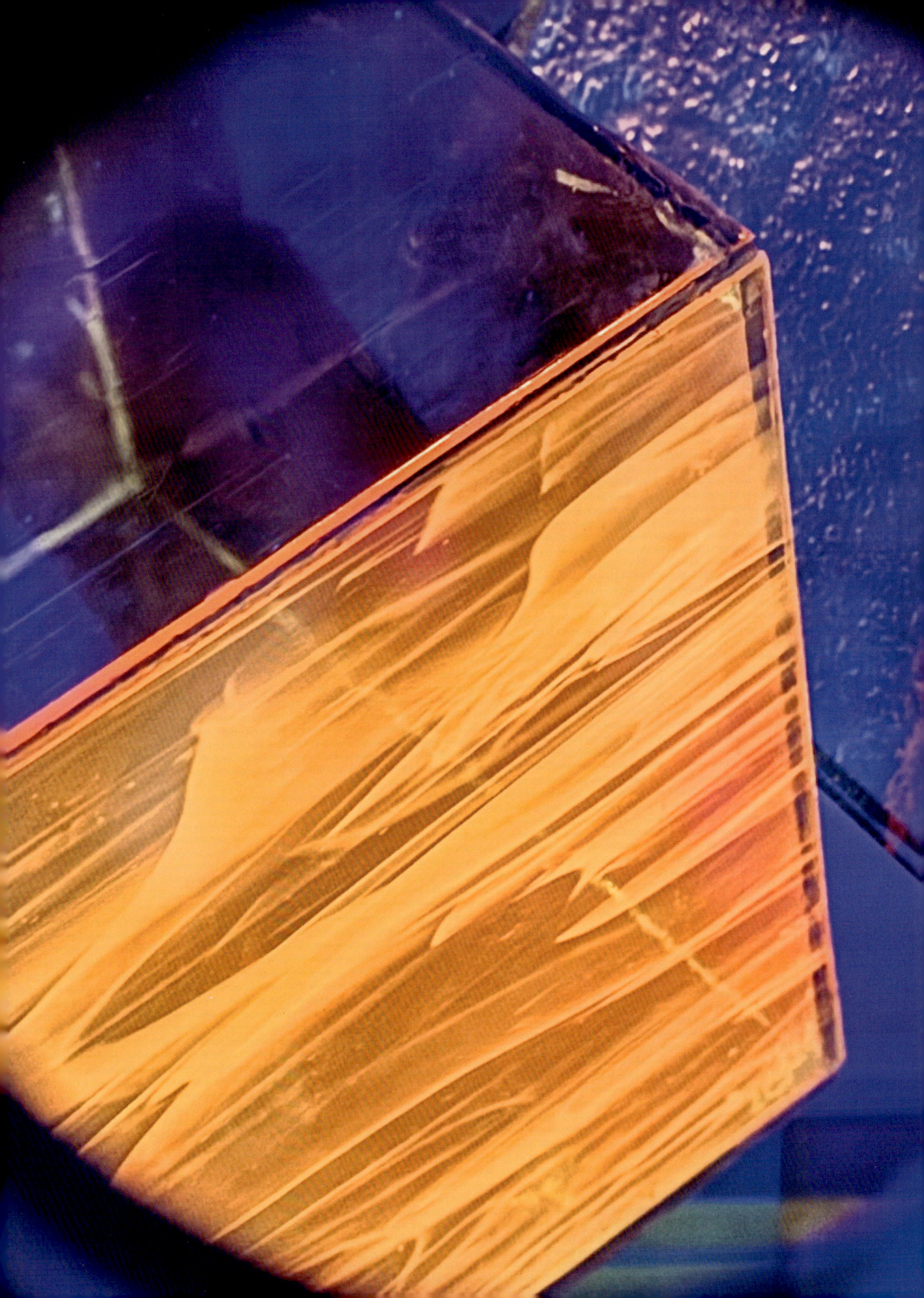

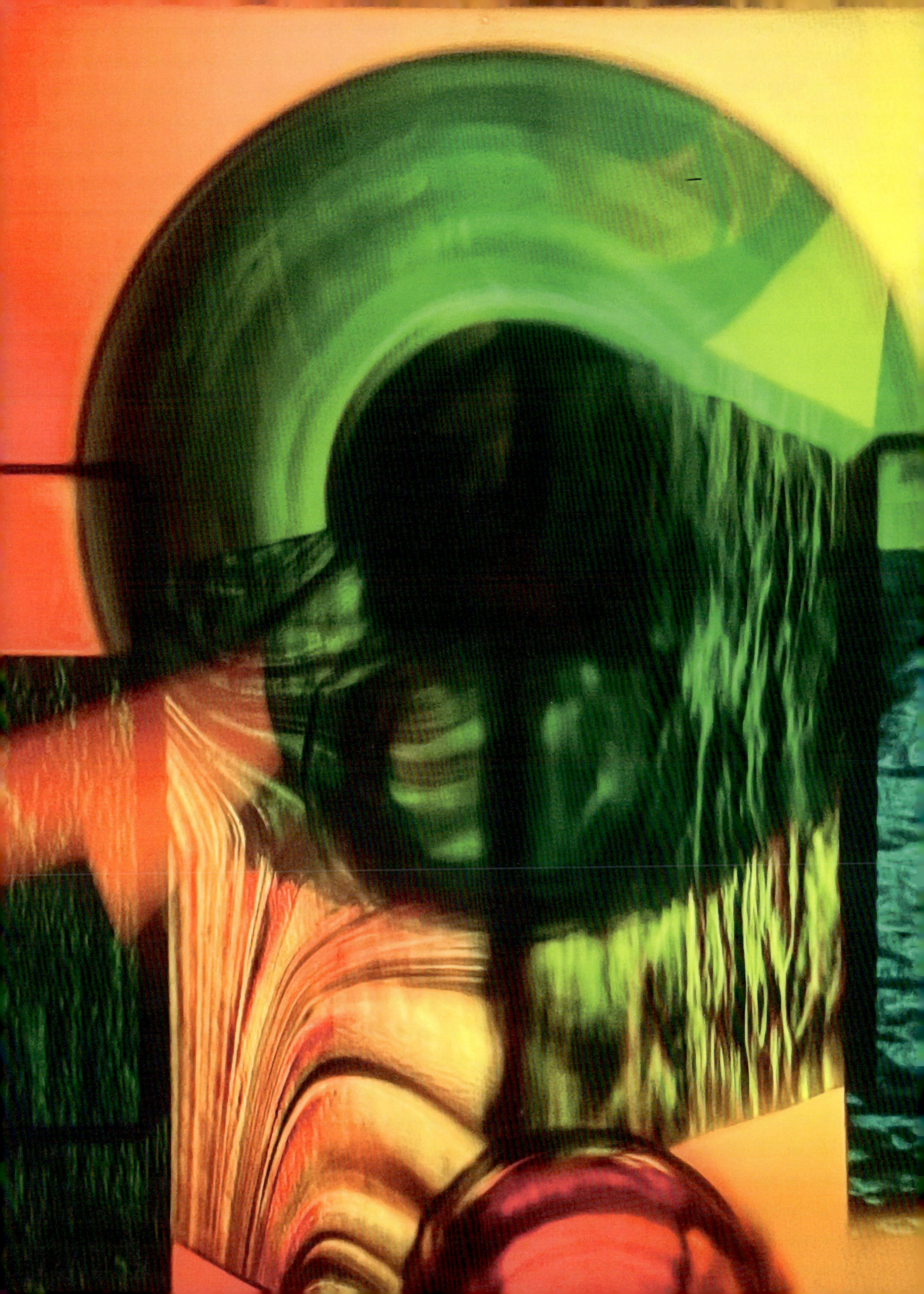

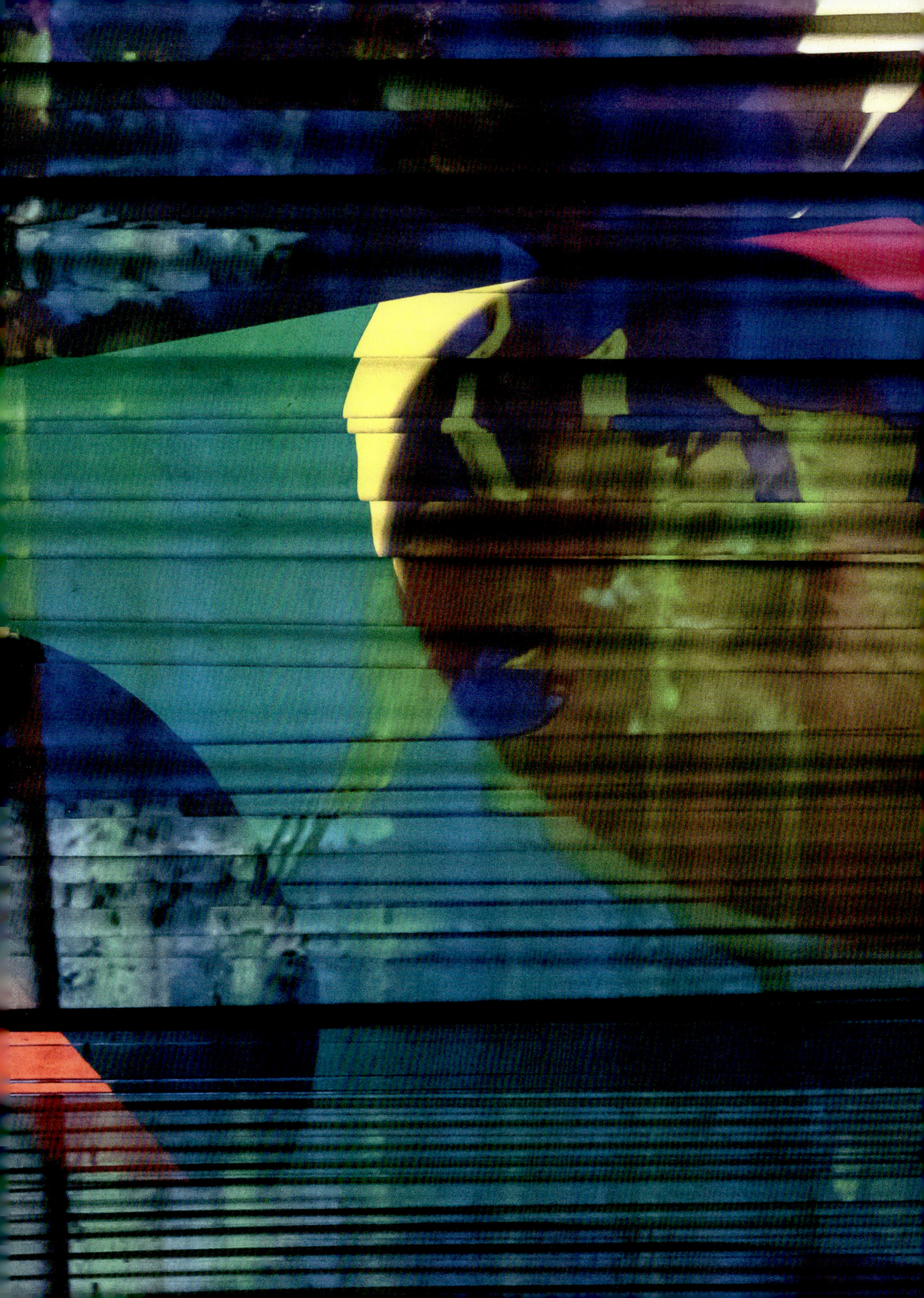

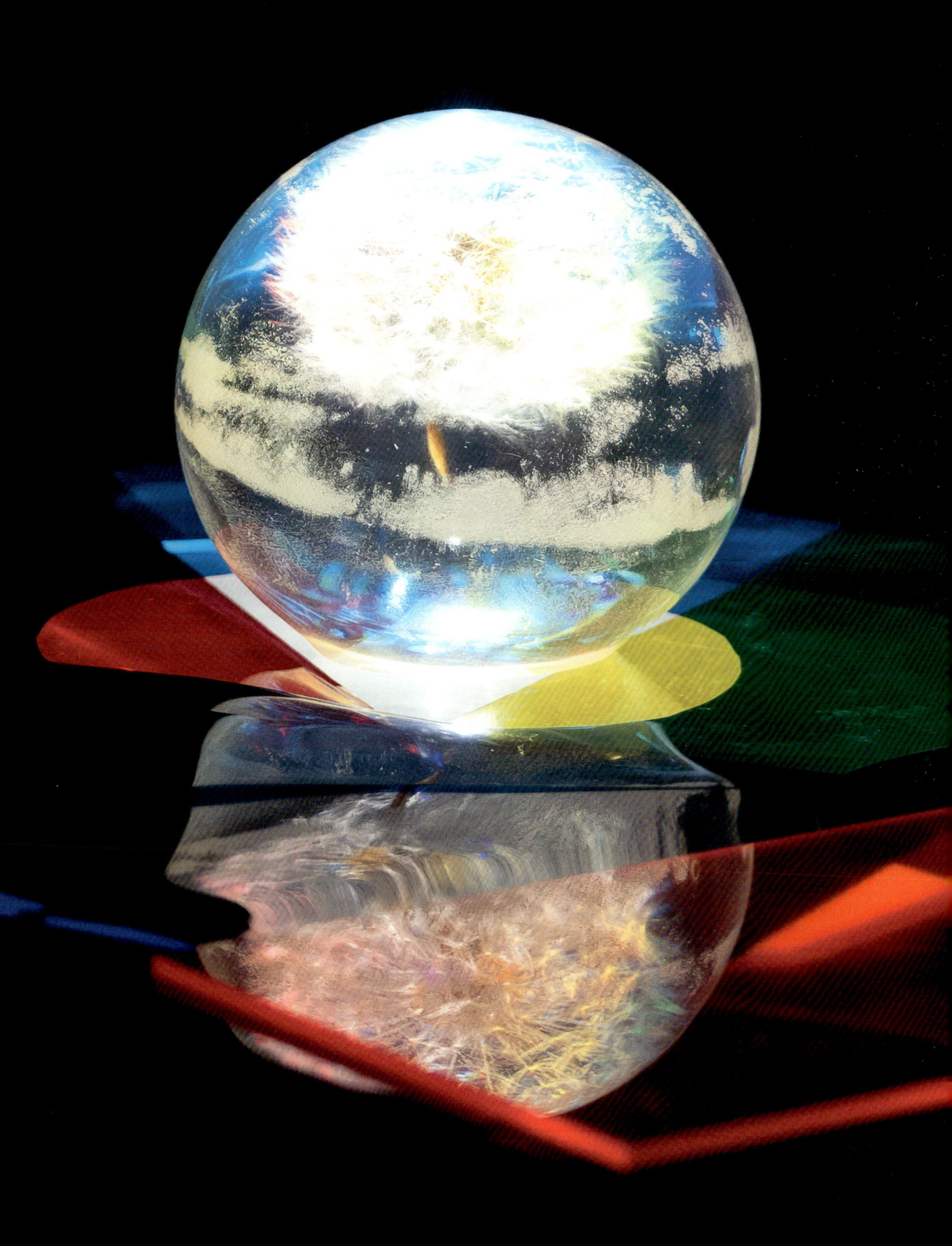

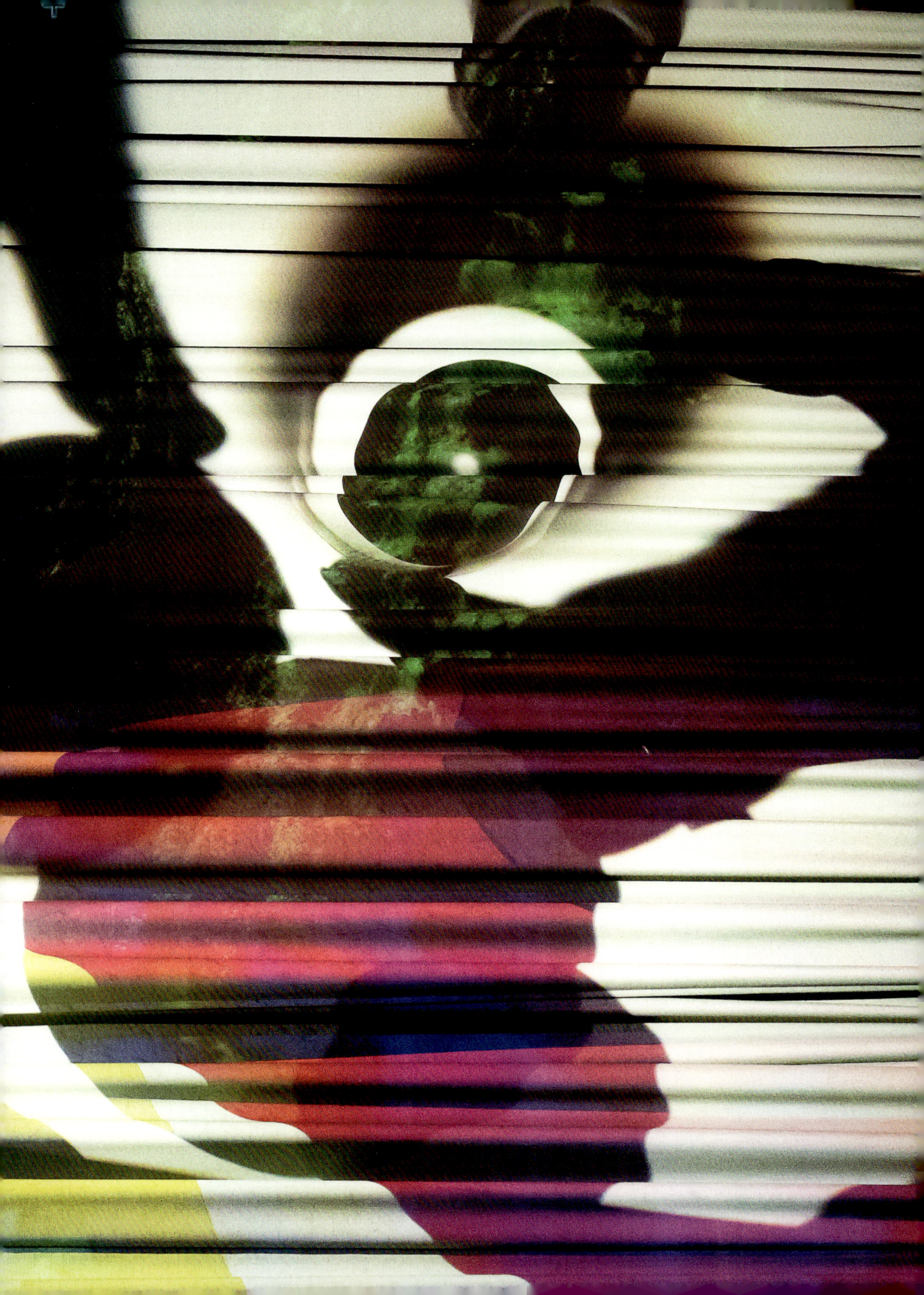

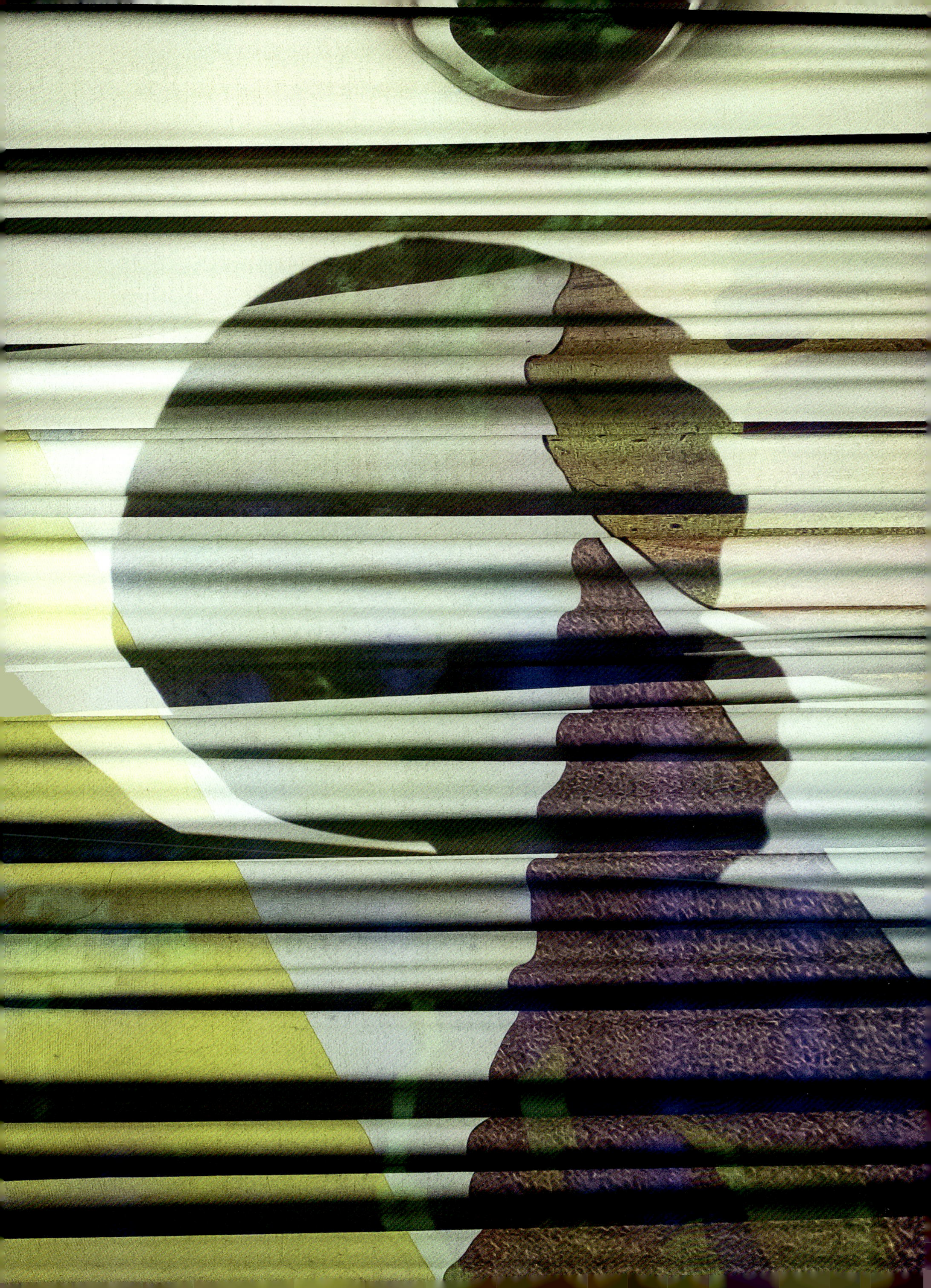

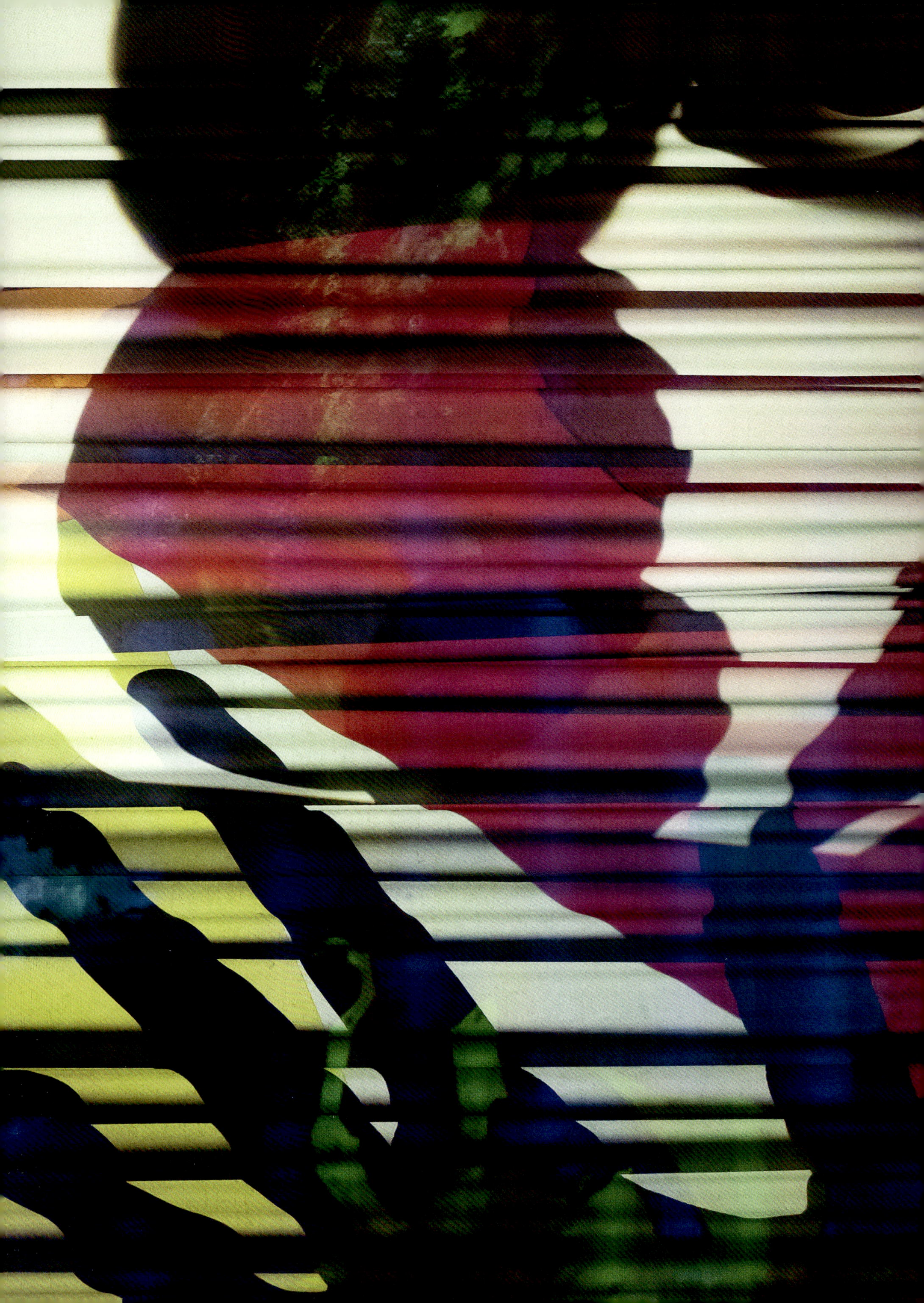

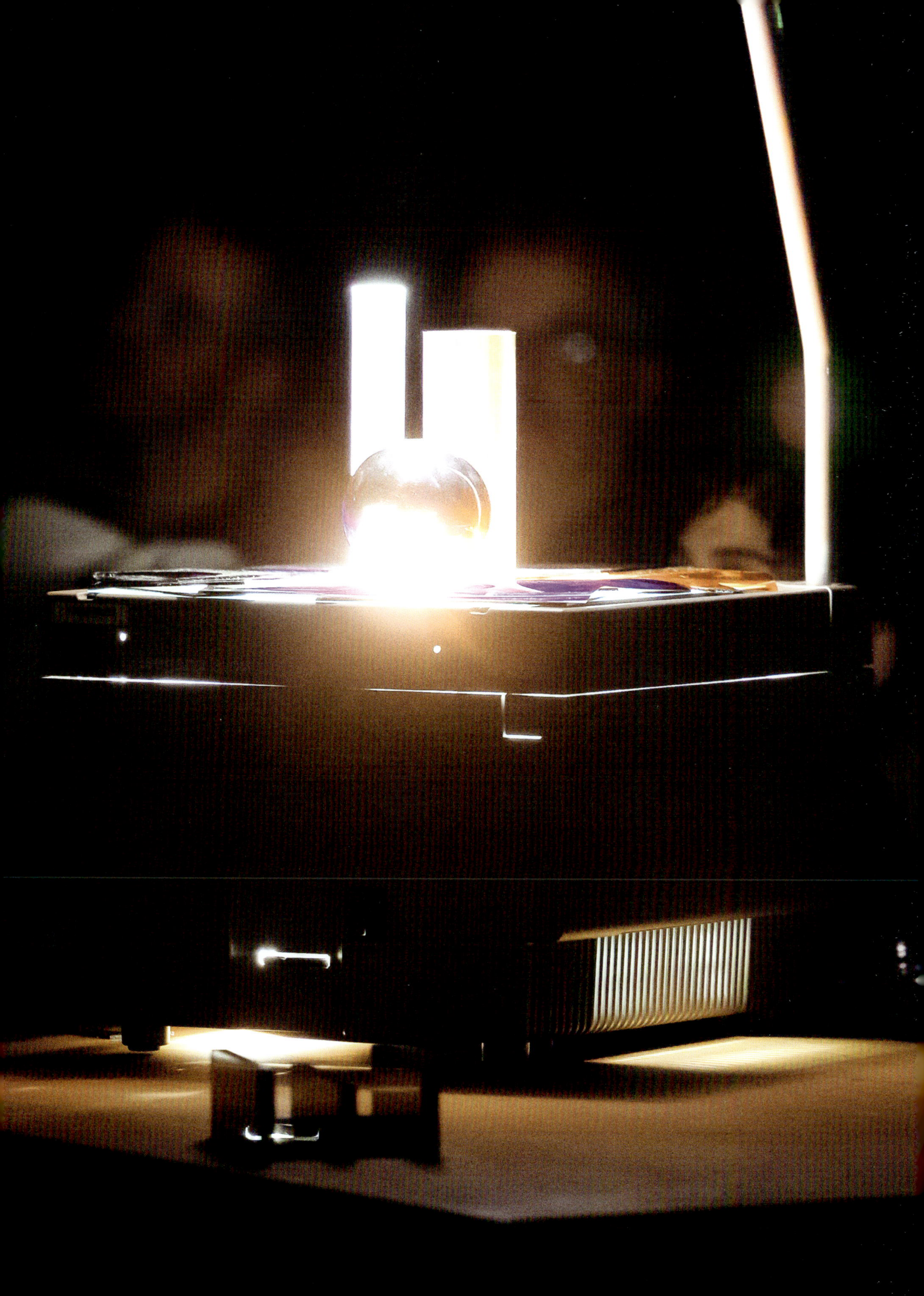

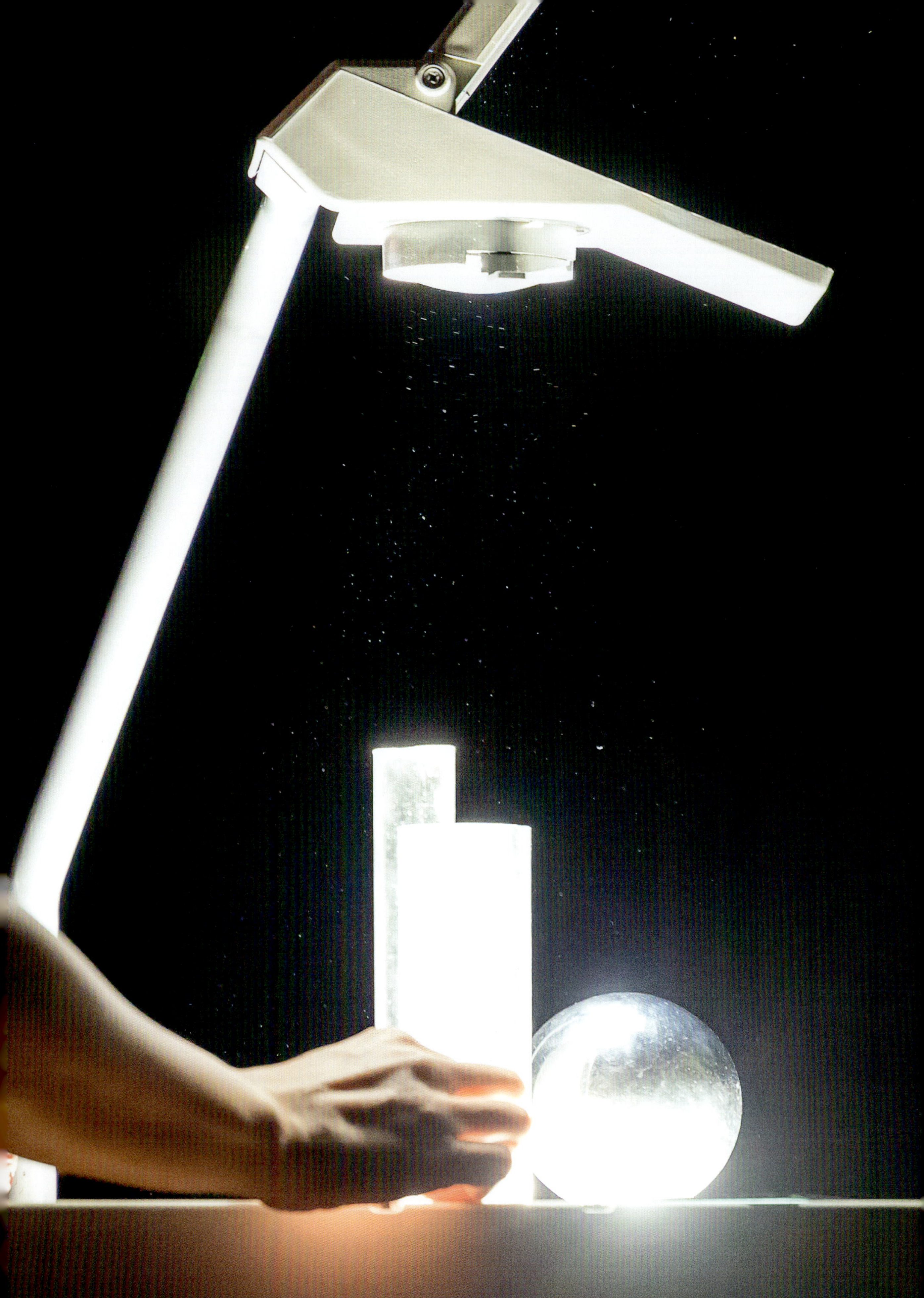

I've been obsessed with windows—windows as an architectural element. They kind of imply, let's say openness, right?

But in fact, the subject inside always has the power or the control over this openness. One can put a shade, open it, let the movement of air or light come in or out. Even if it is closed, the transparency infuses the image or idea of openness, but it's not actually open. The transparency and the see-through effect falsely convey approachability. So there's this open, transparent thing that actually is a full-on border, it's a wall.

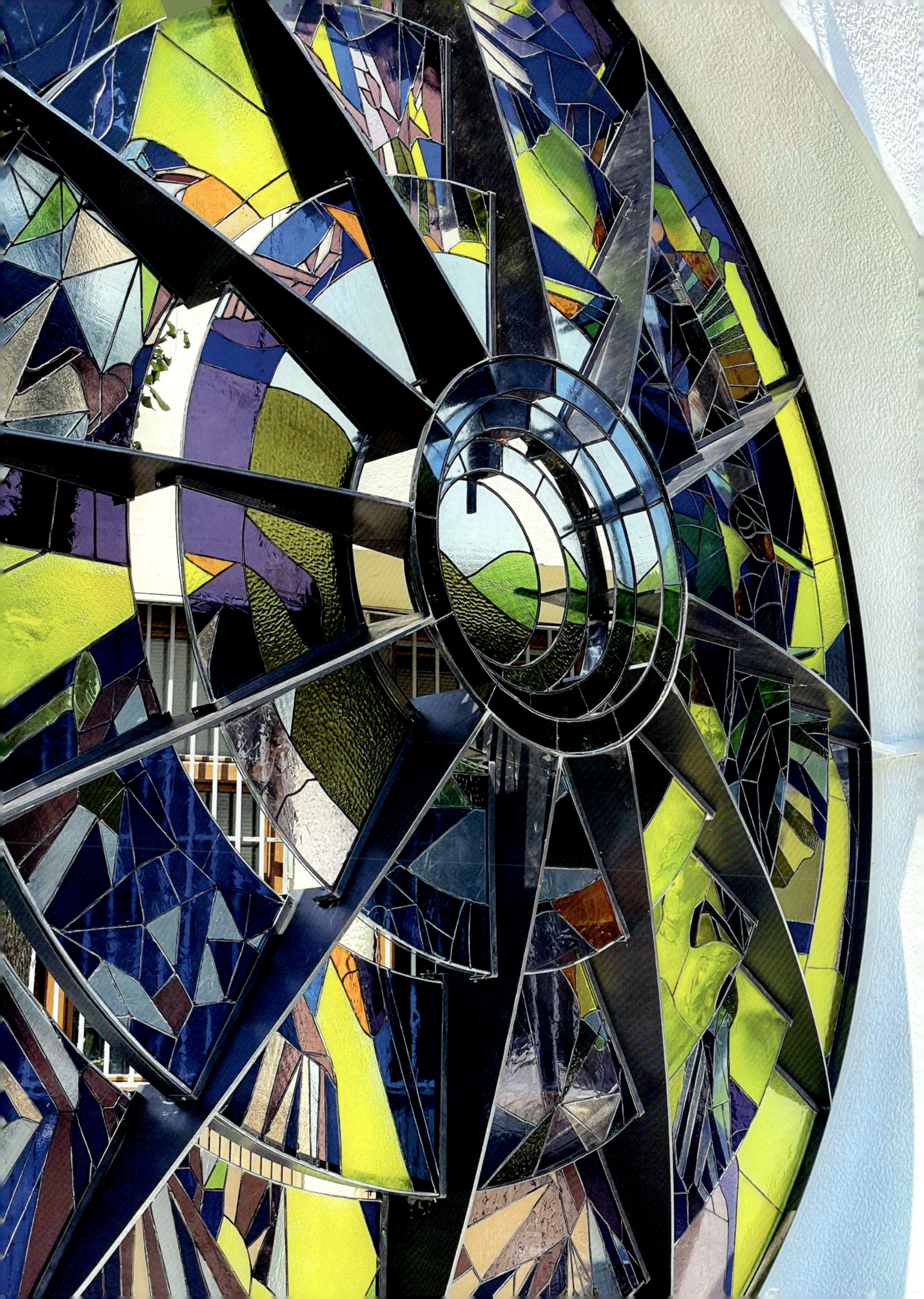

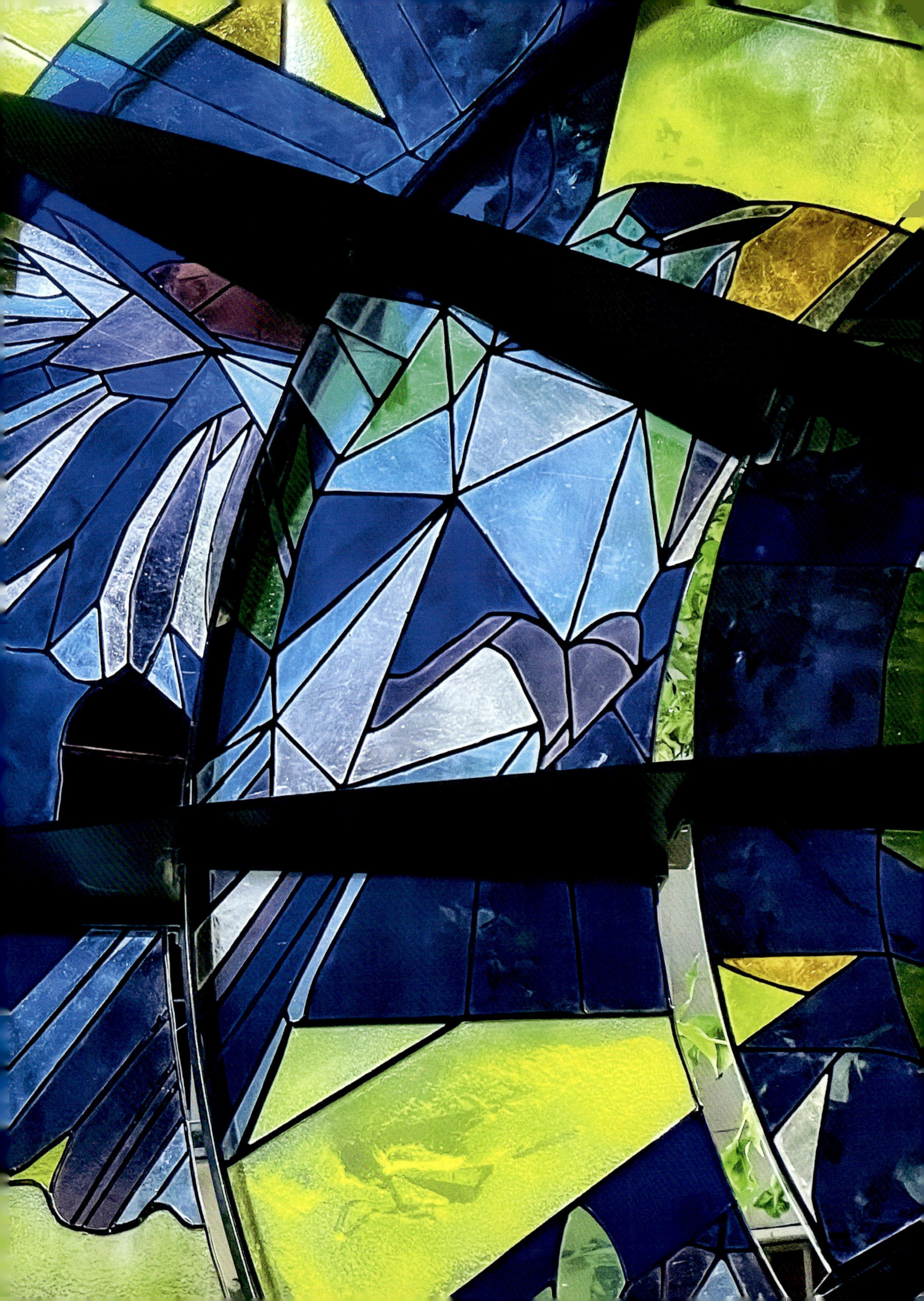

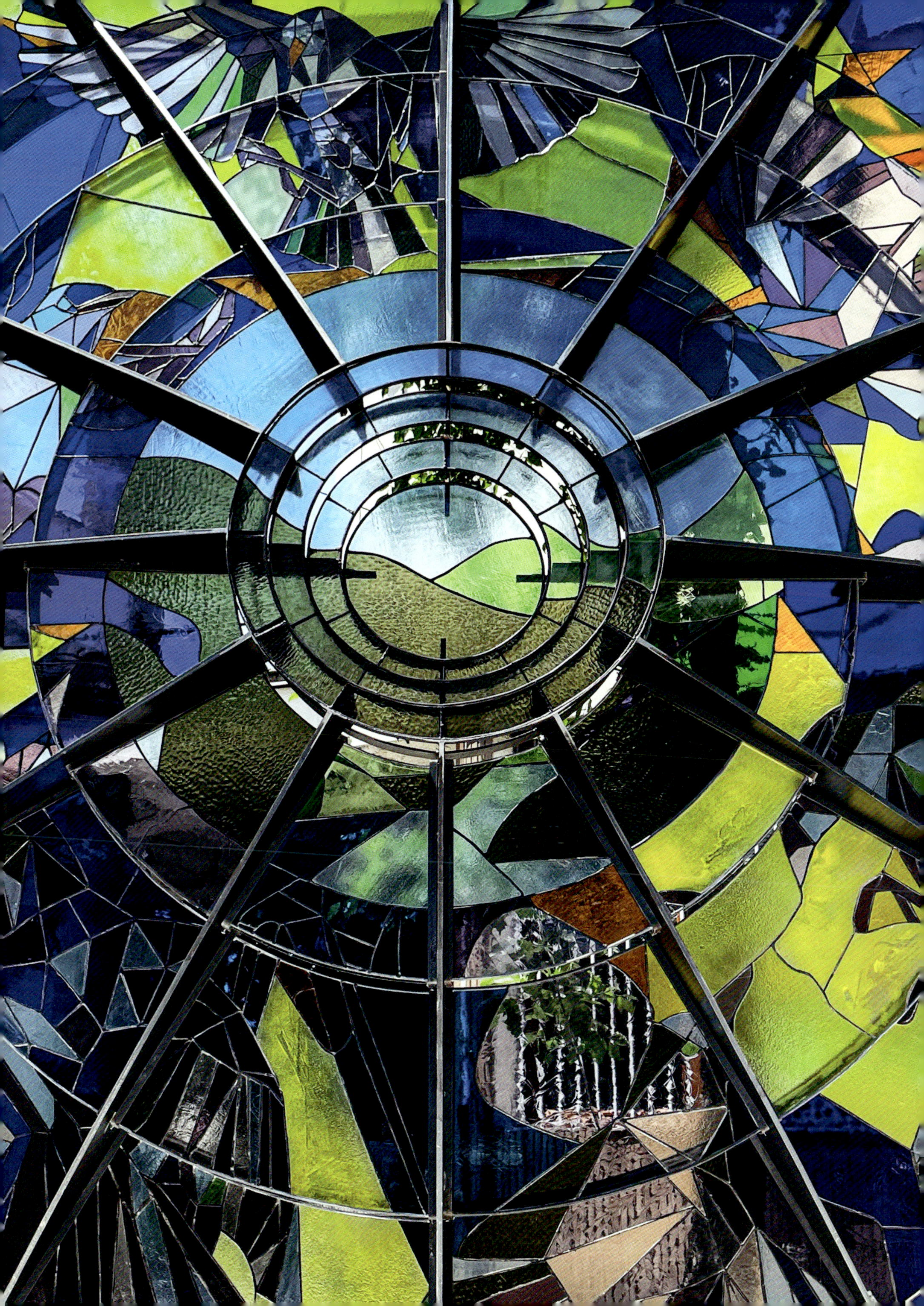

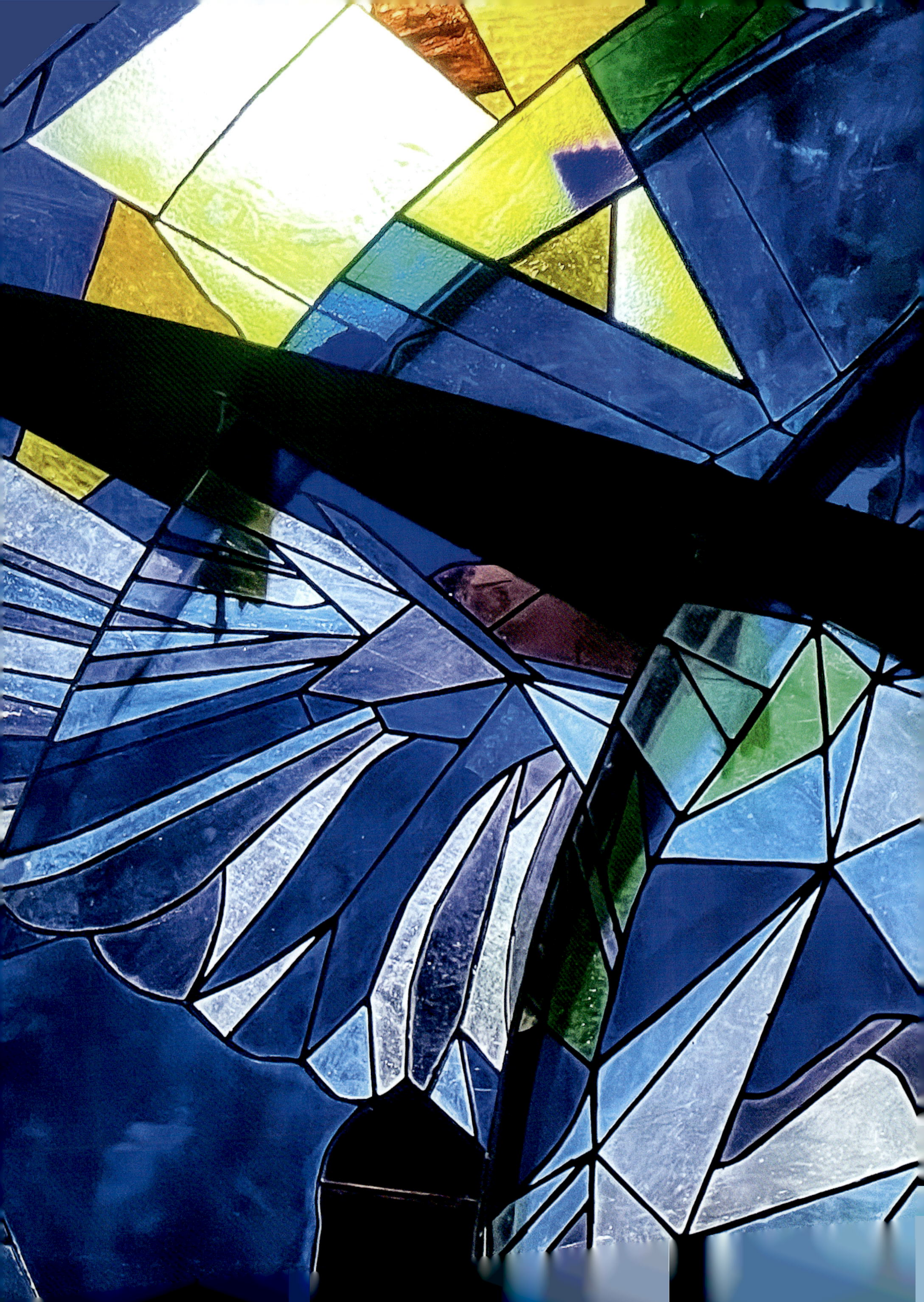

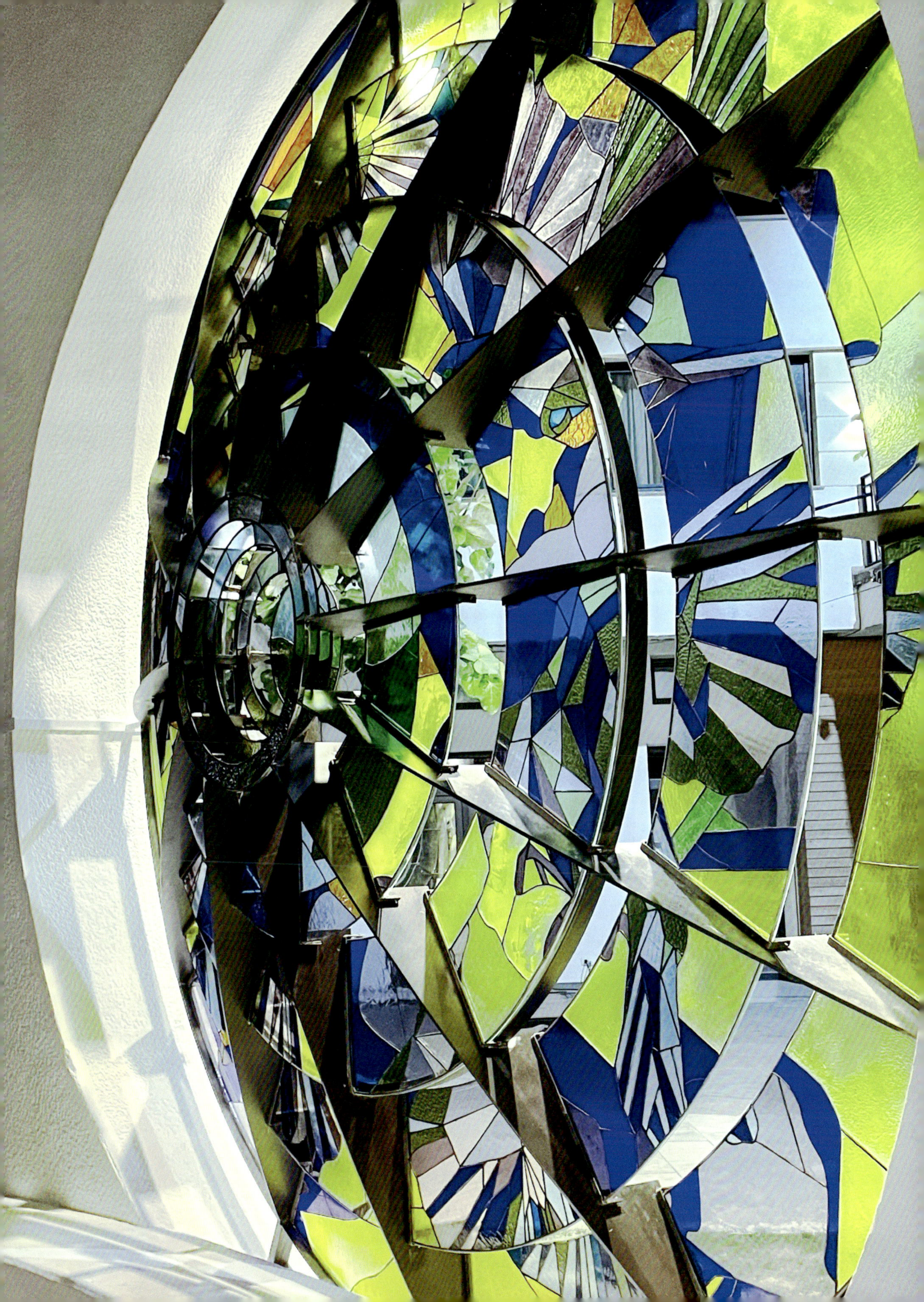

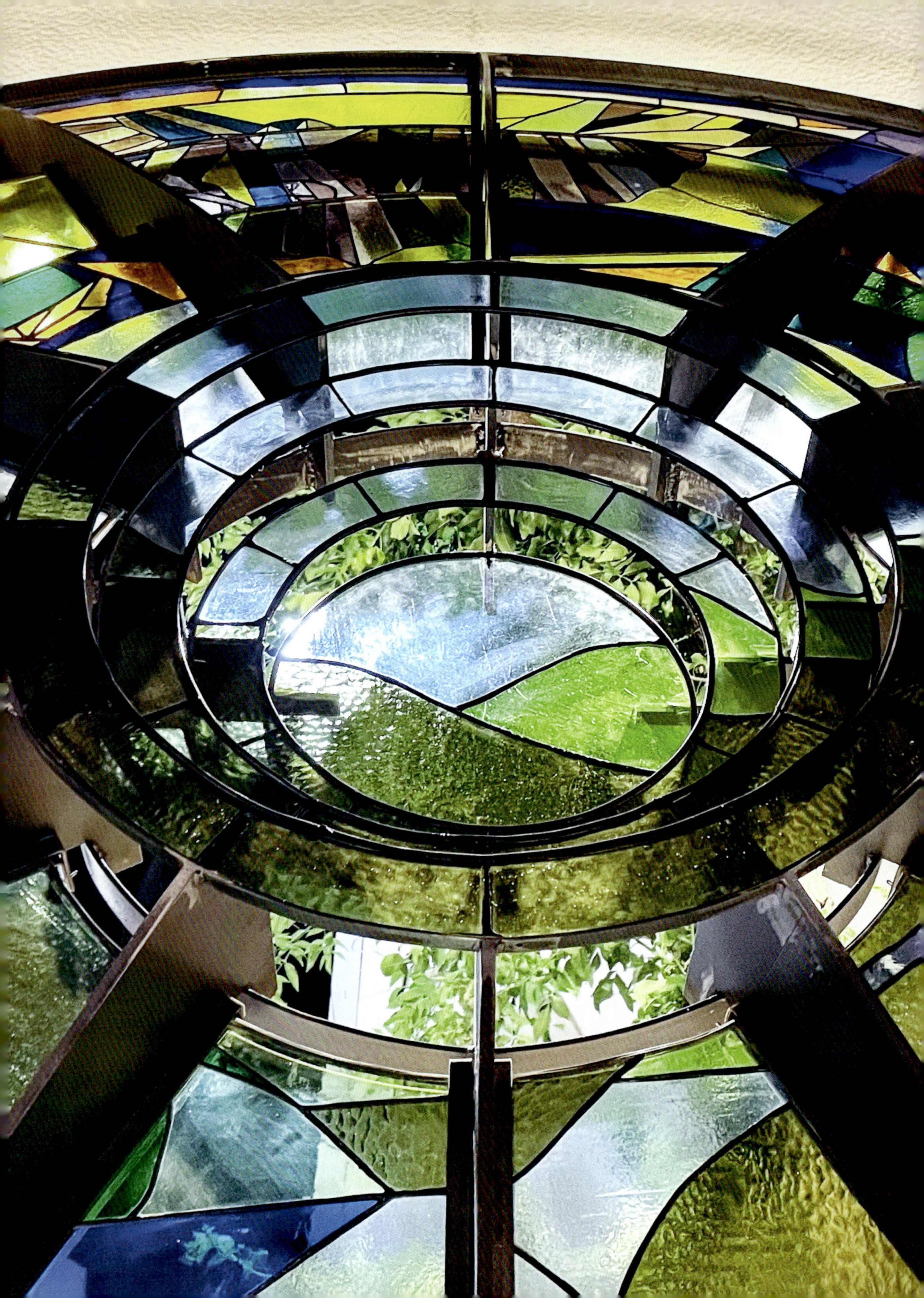

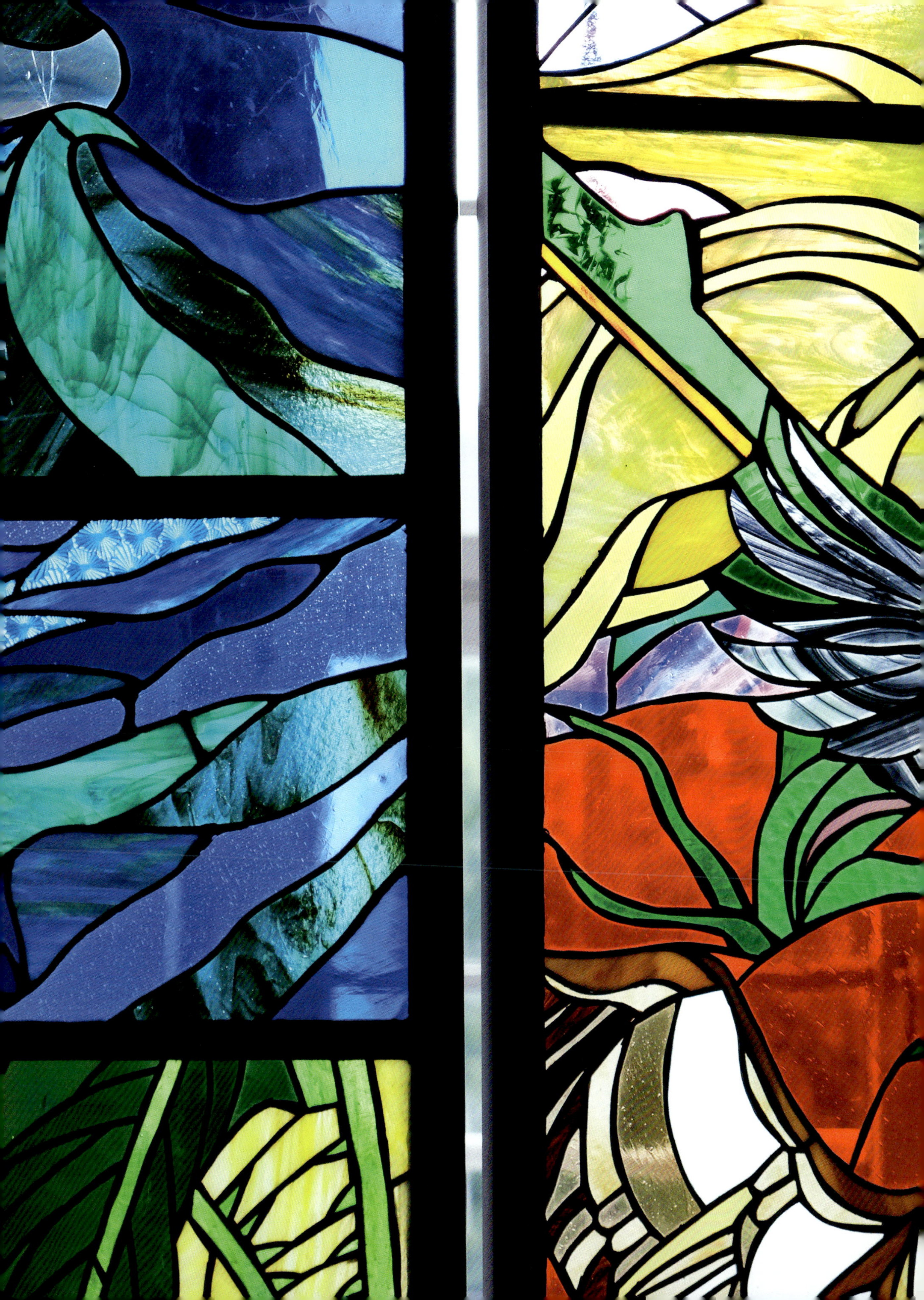

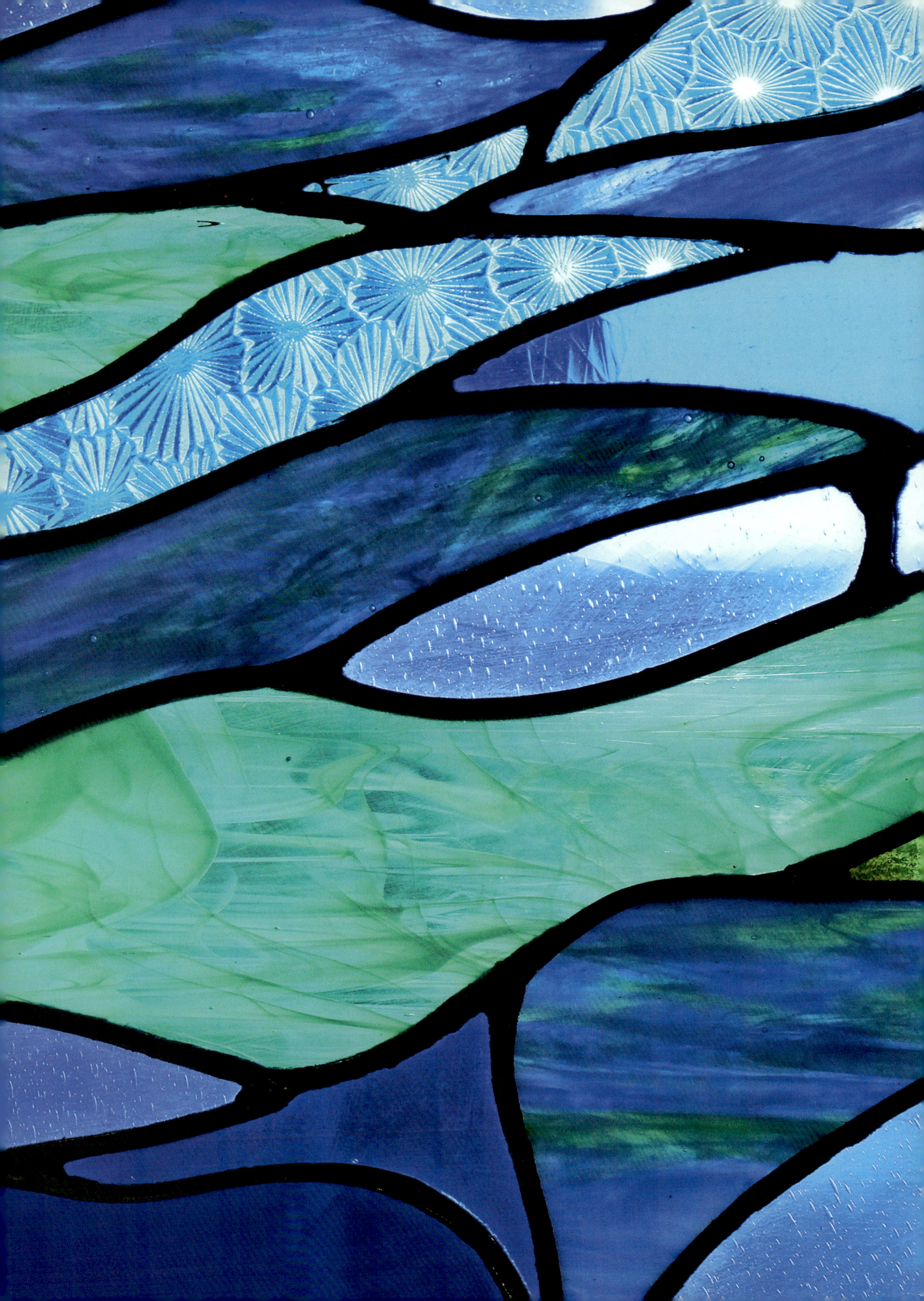

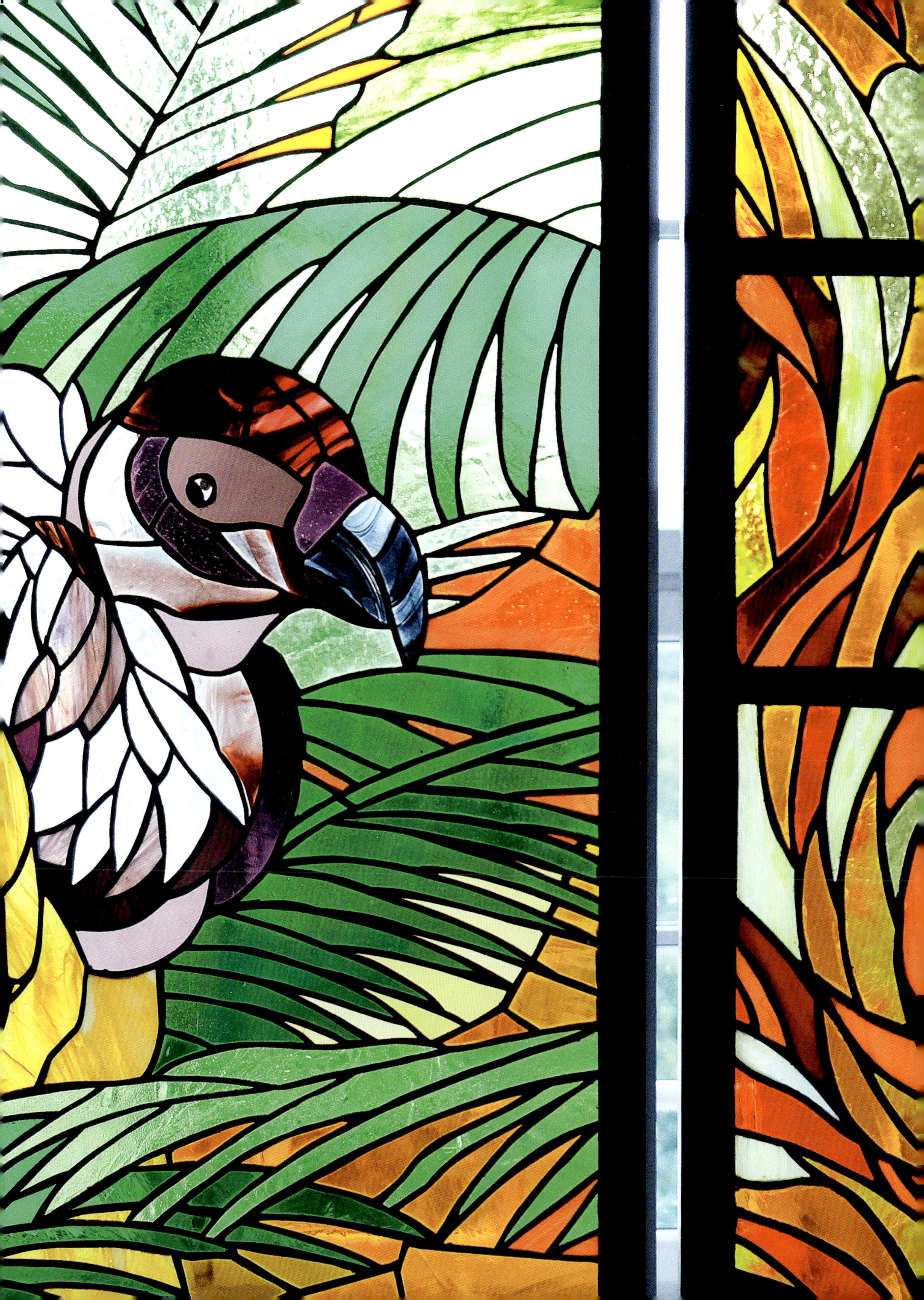

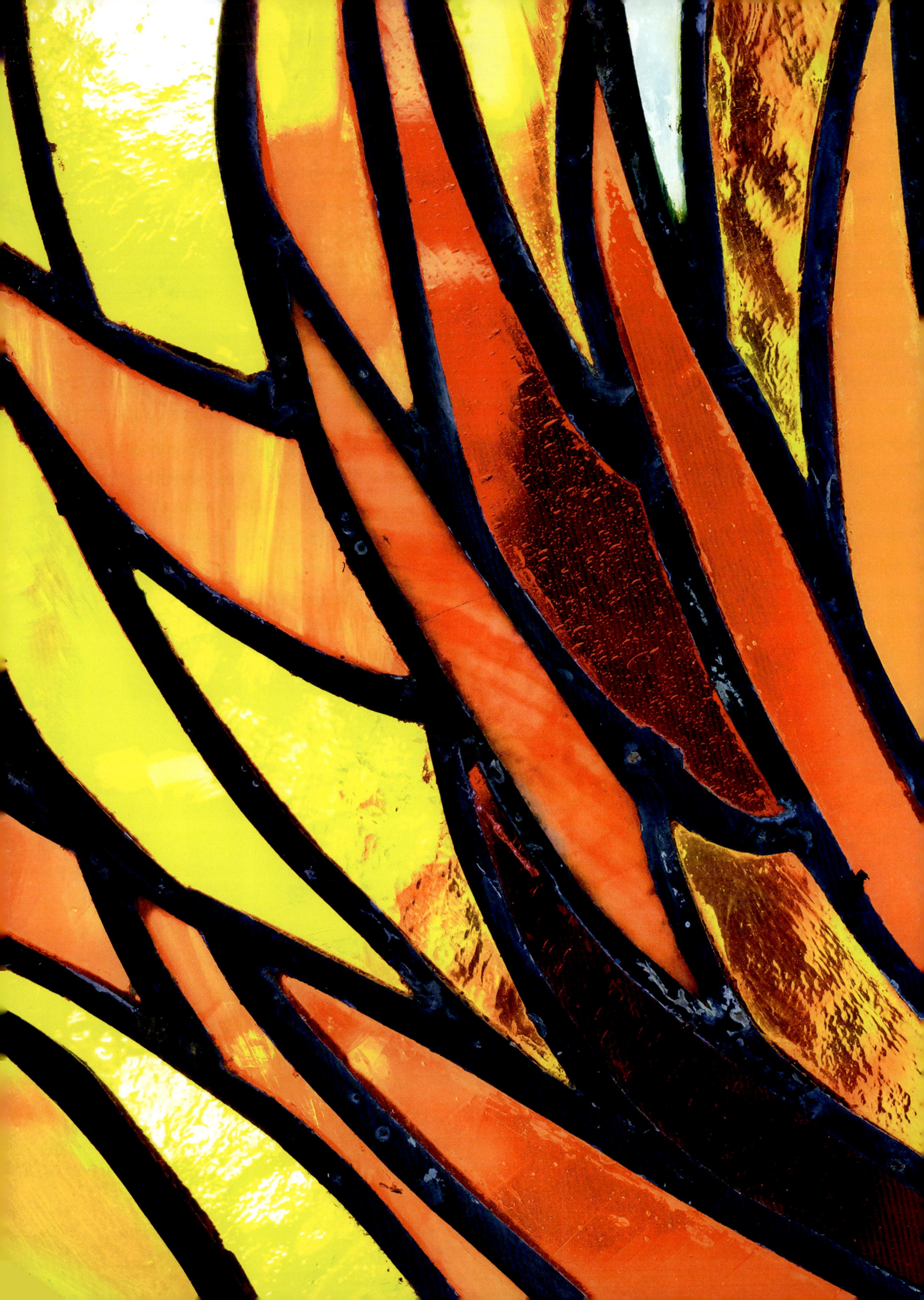

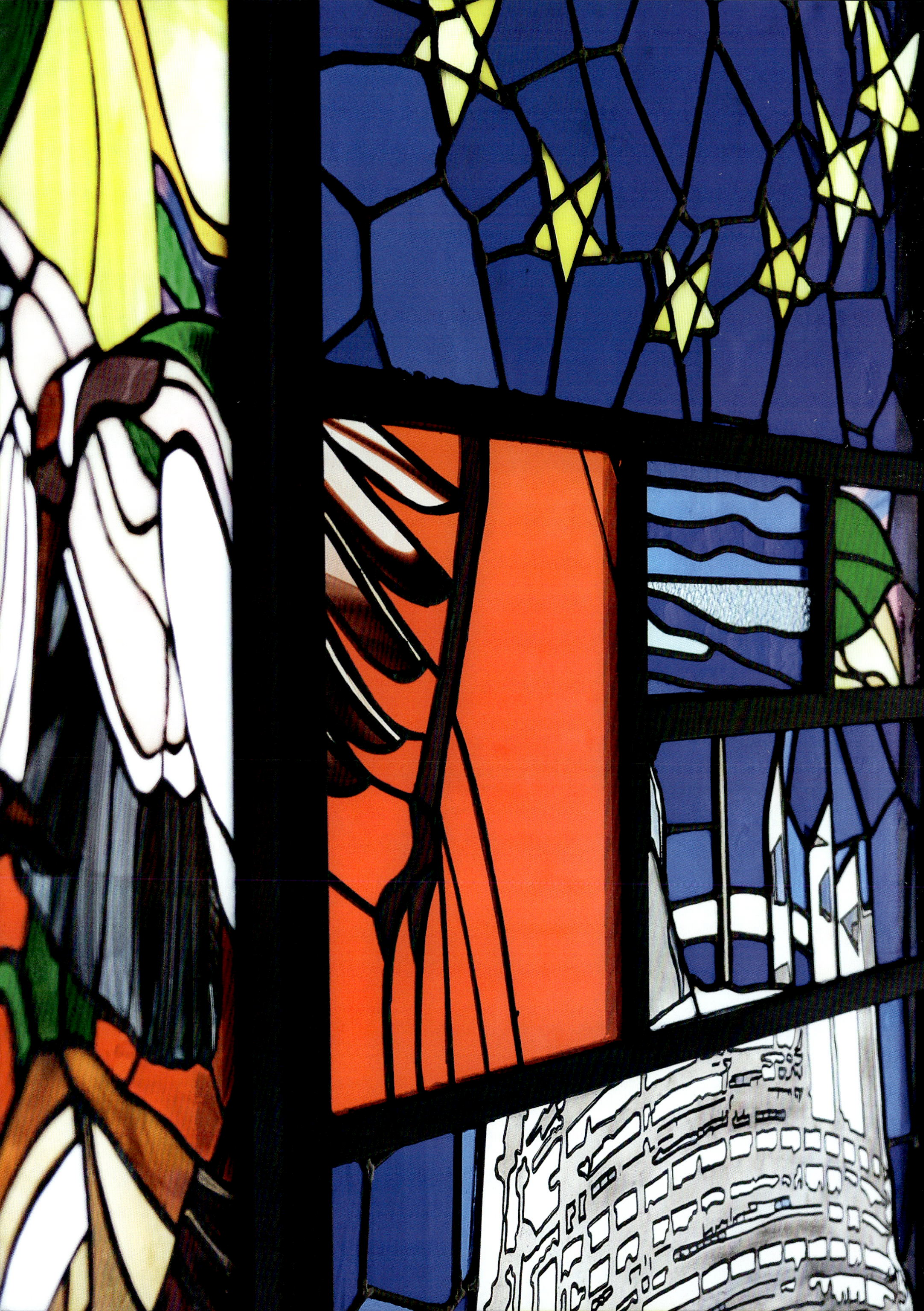

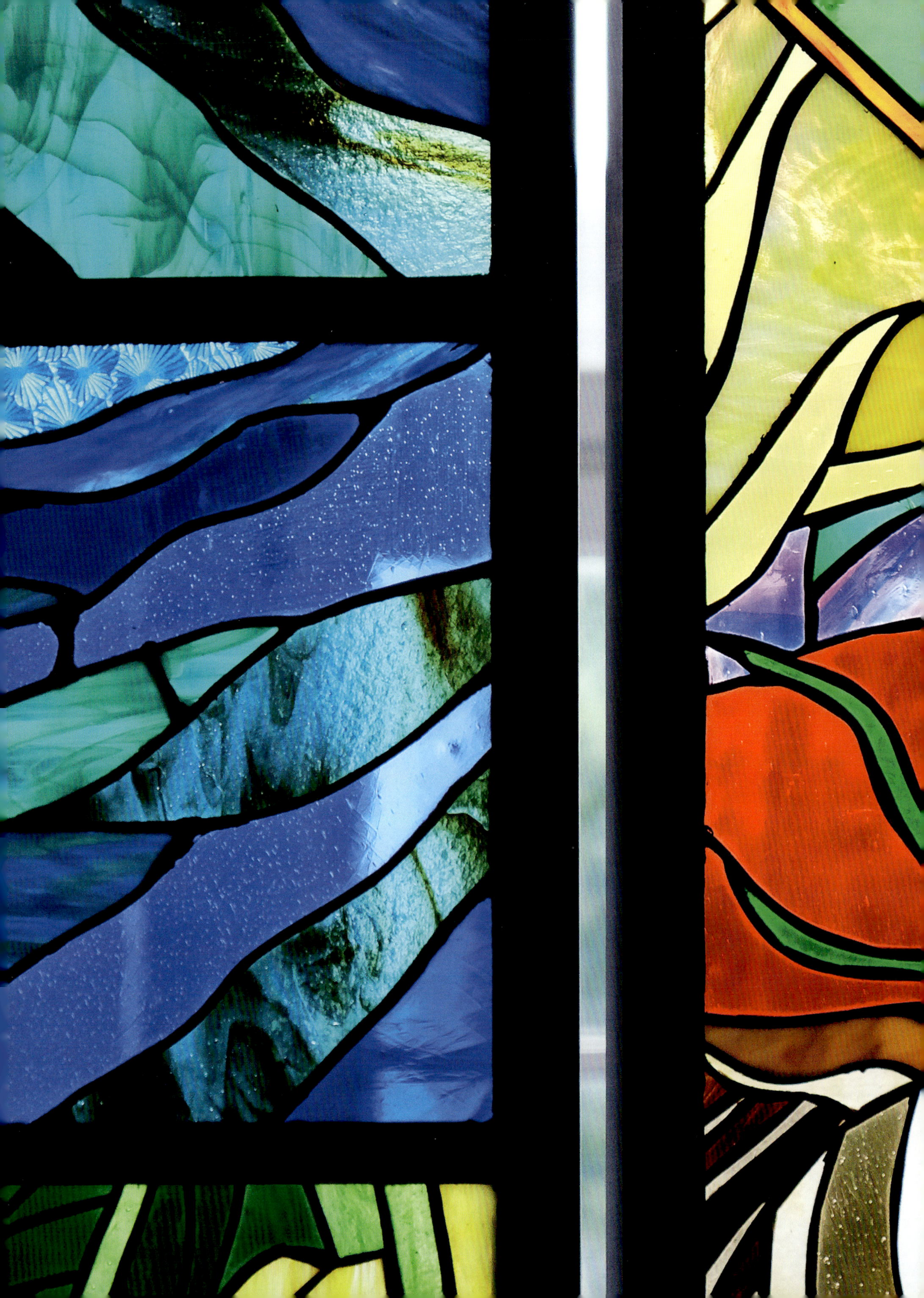

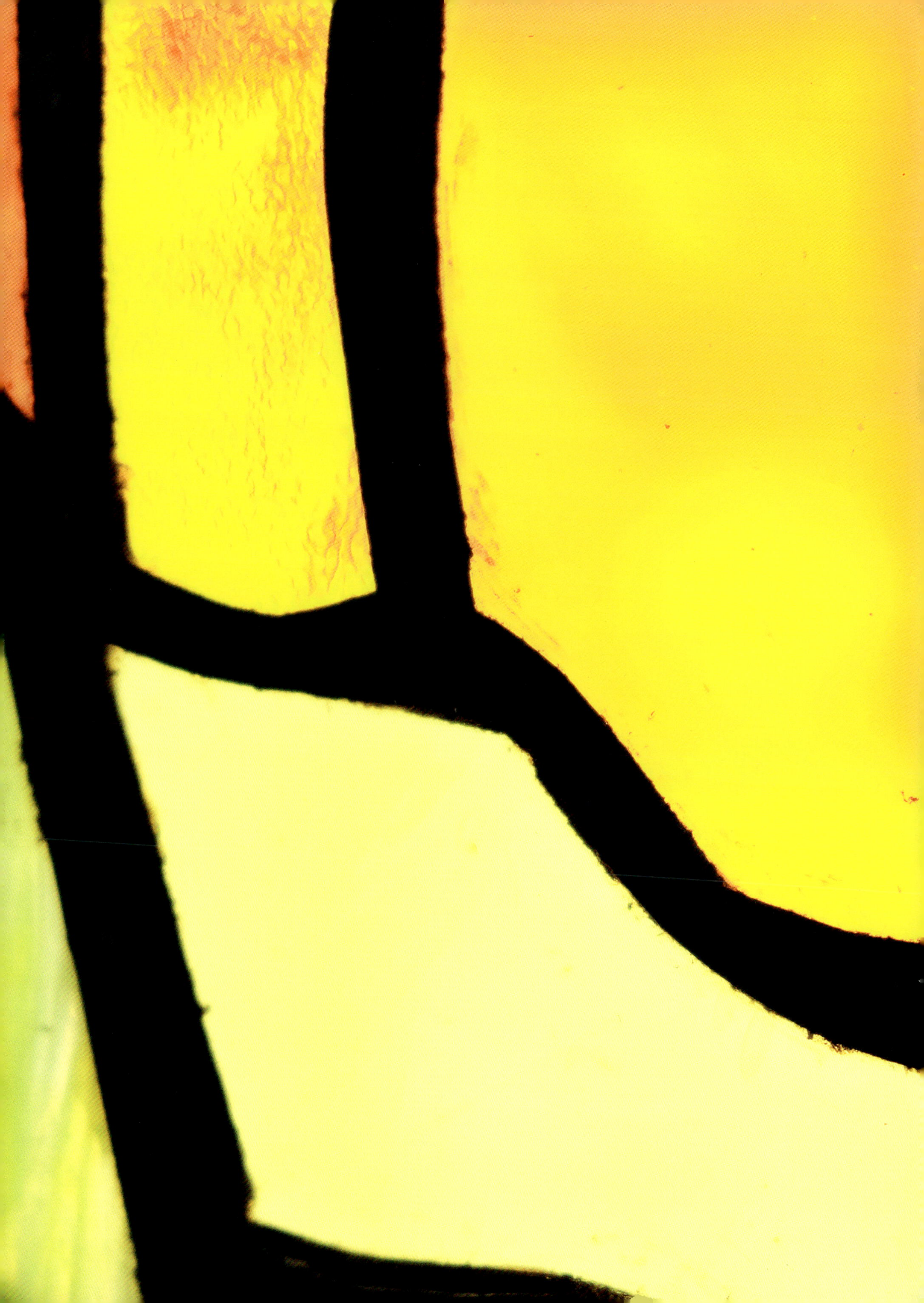

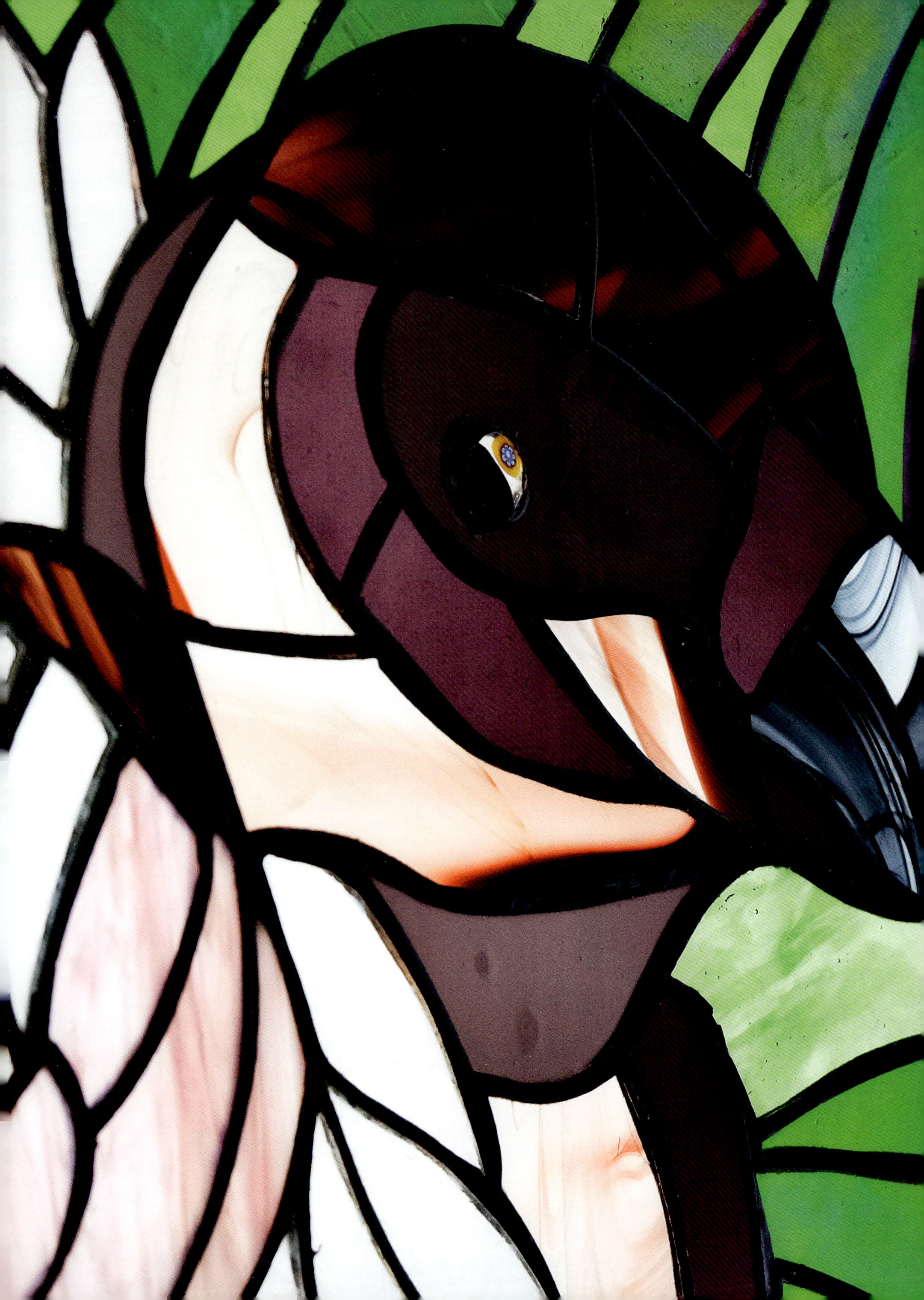

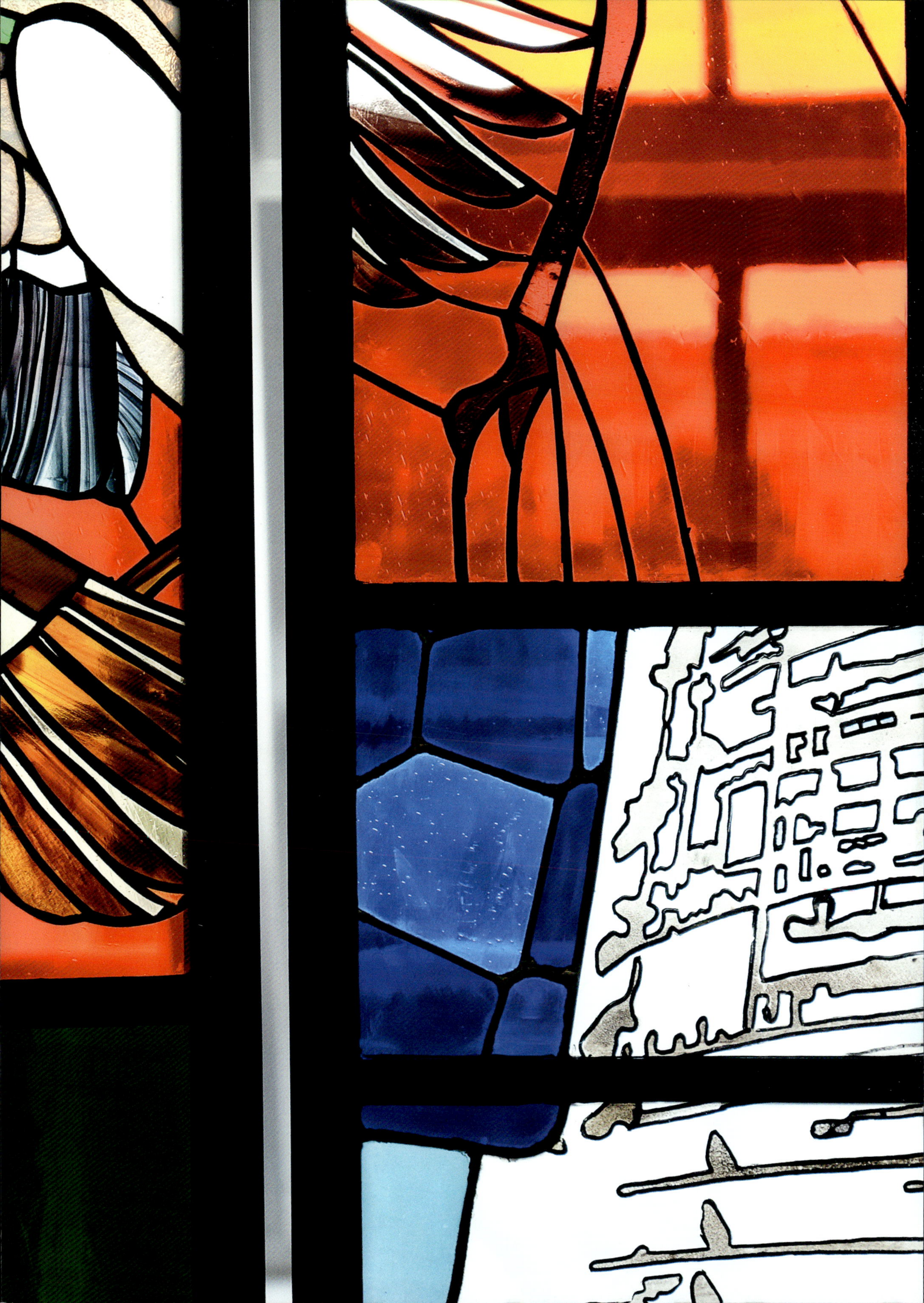

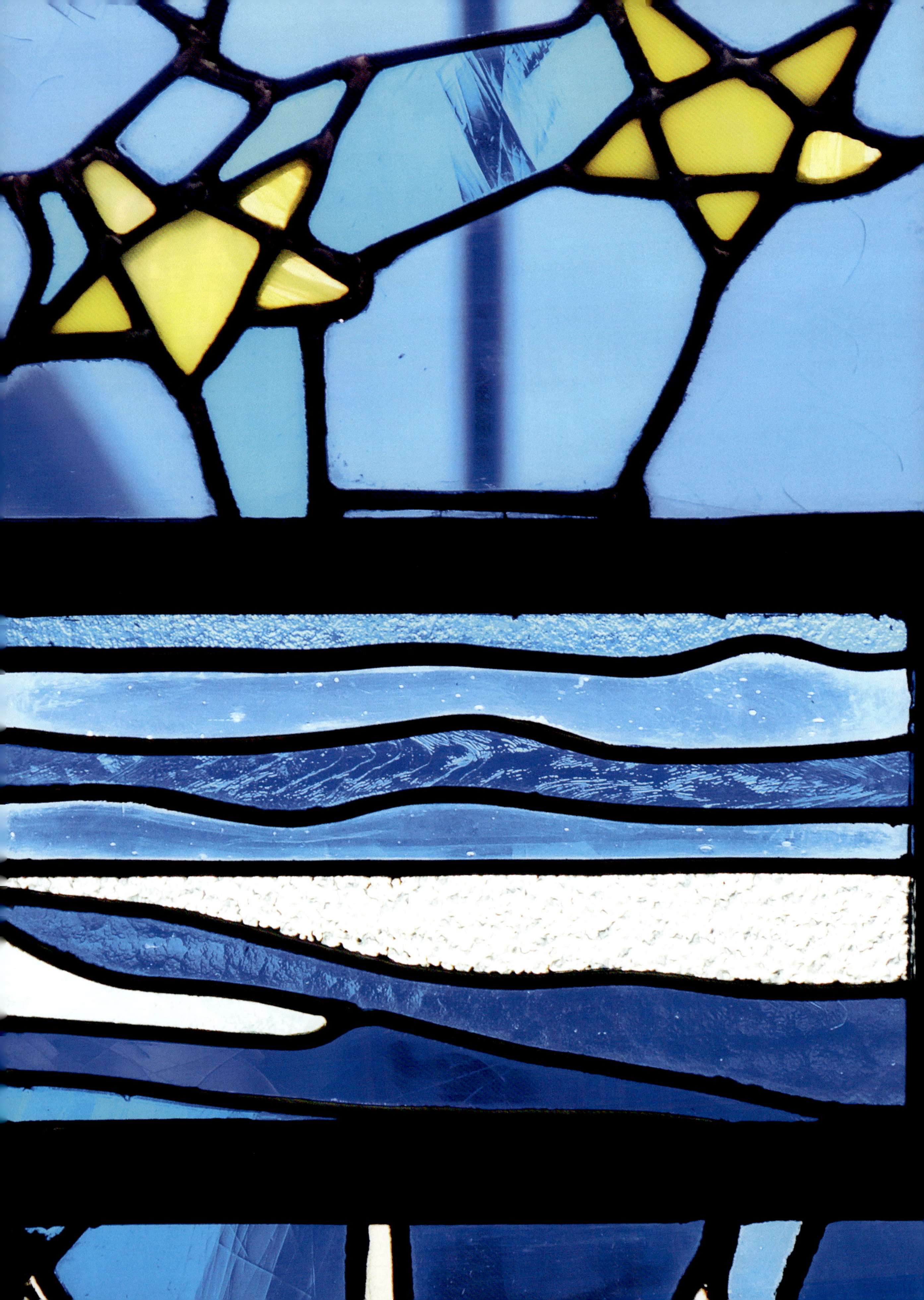

WORKS

2018–2024

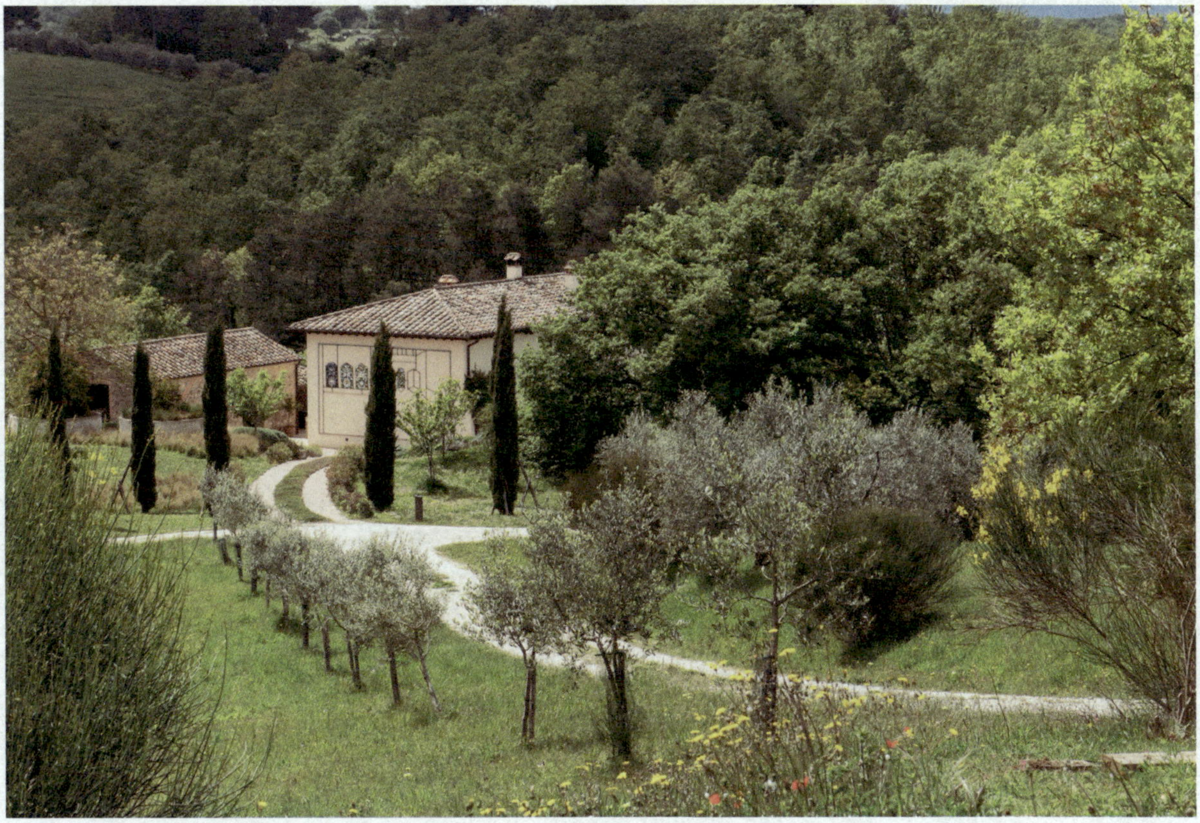

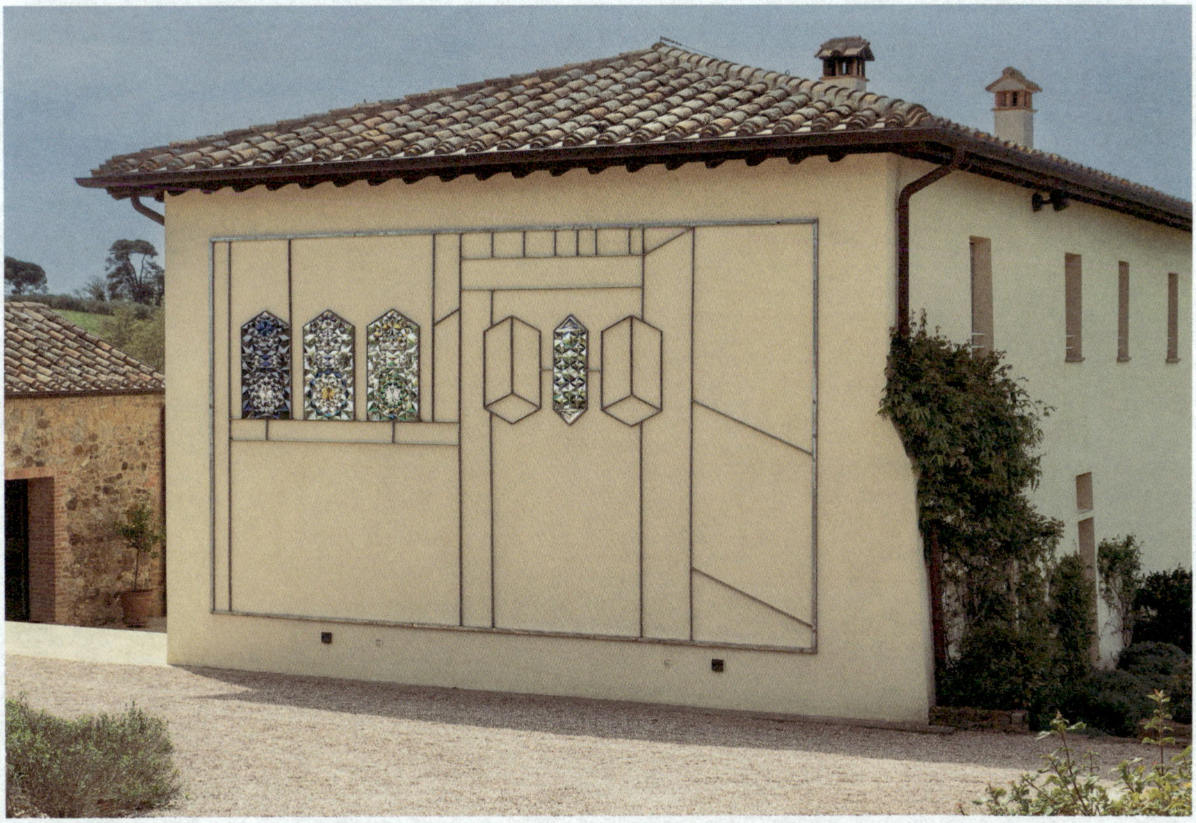

Whispers Across Horizons, 2024
Mirror wall sculptures, stainless steel structure
Podere Trafonti

In the Depth of the Night, Sky Sees the Sun, 2023
Stained glass, stainless steel structure
League Square, Prizren

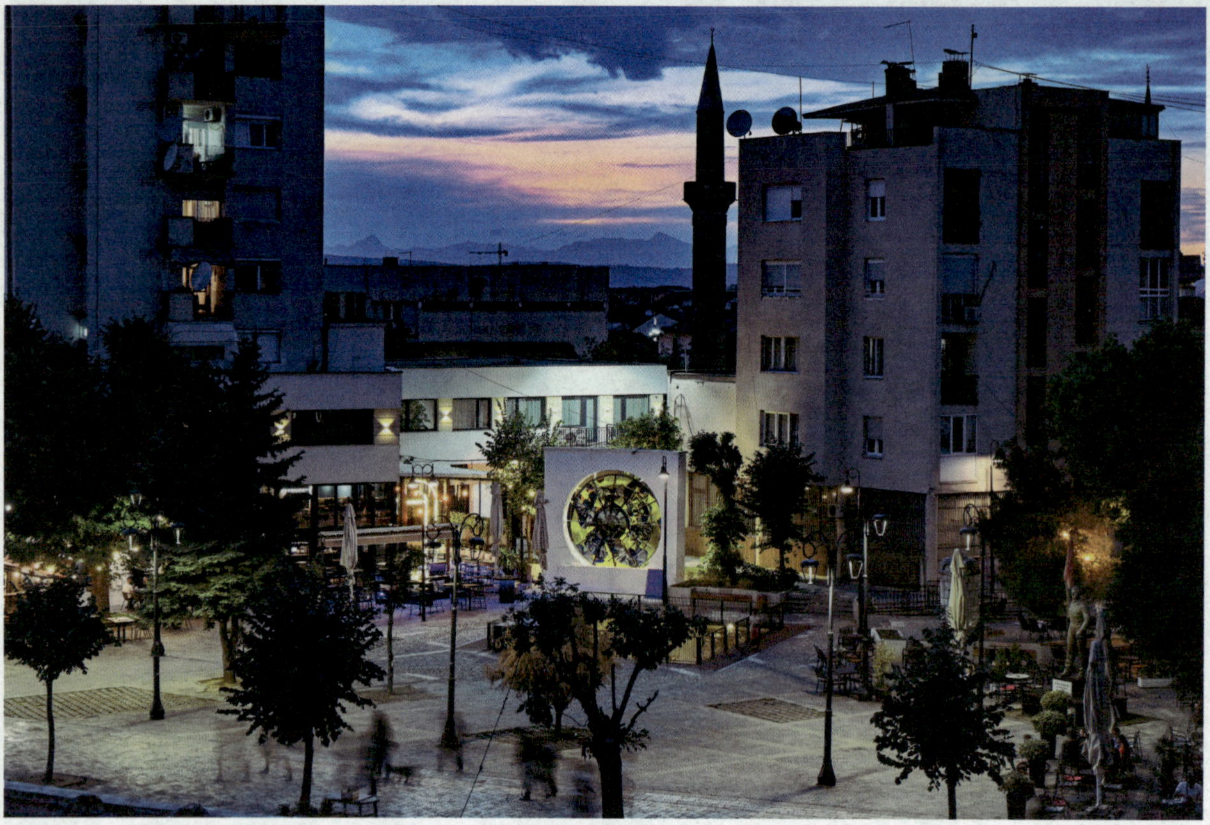

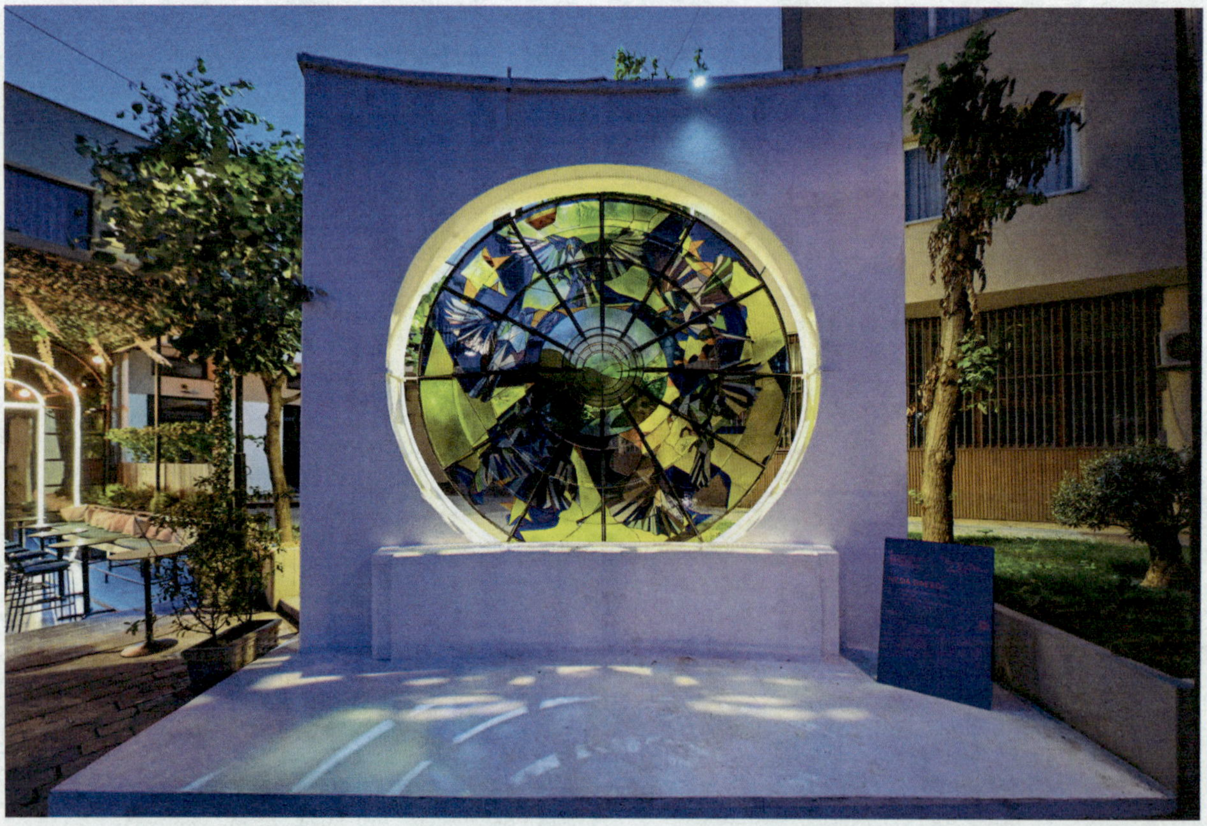

In the Depth of the Night, Sterile Steel, 2022
Stained glass, stainless steel structure
League Square, Prizren

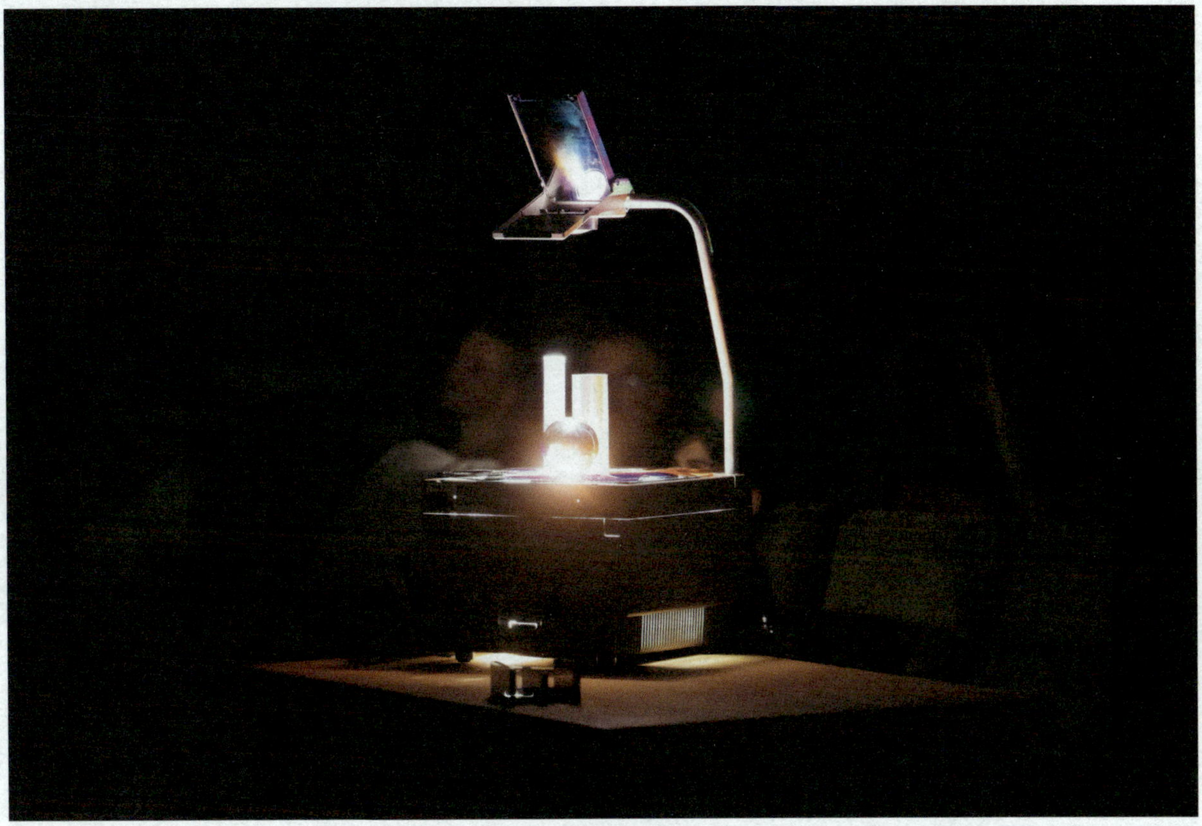

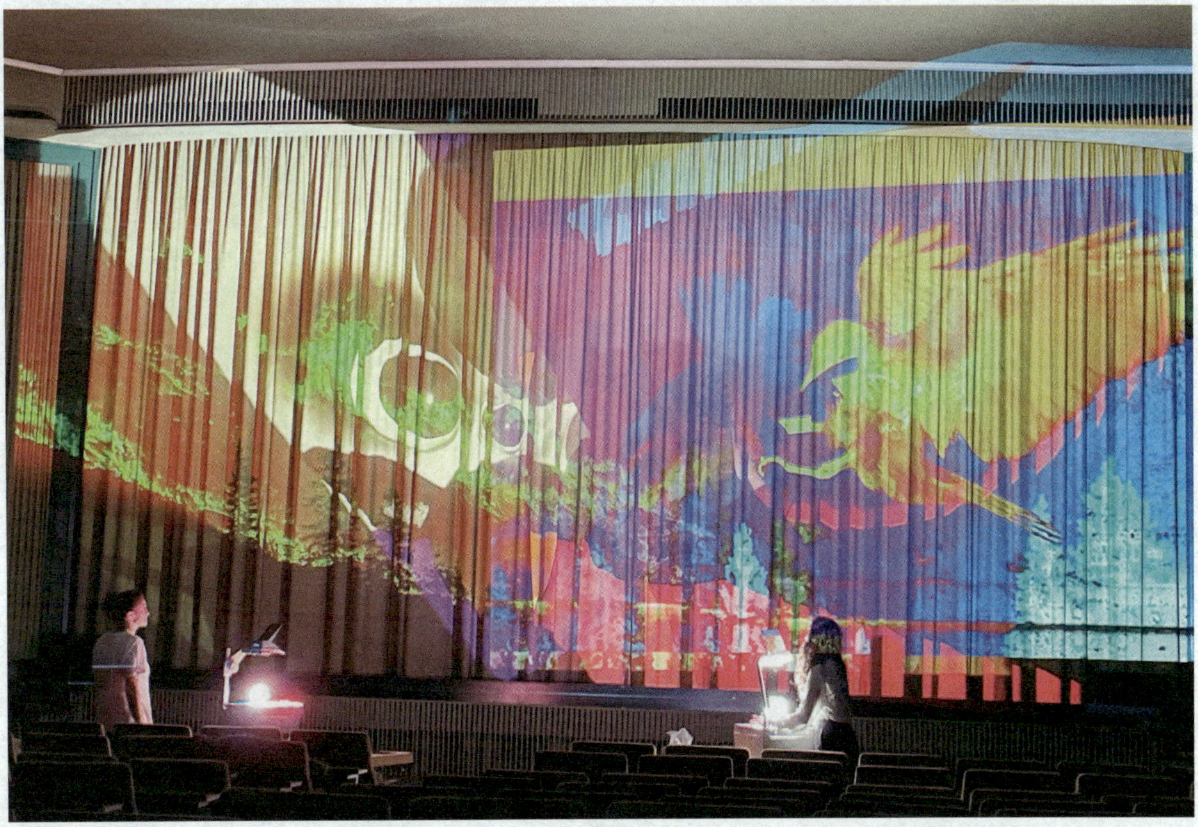

Sunsets Are Not Overrated, 2022
In collaboration with Setareh Shahbazi
Projection performance
On the occasion of lumbung Film - AFTER CINEMA at documenta fifteen, Gloria Kino Kassel

Sunsets Are Not Overrated, 2022
in collaboration with Setareh Shahbazi
Projection-performance
On the occasion of lumbung Film–AFTER CINEMA at documenta fifteen, Gloria Kino Kassel

Only Birds Who Fly the Highest Can Shatter the Windows, 2022
Stained glass, stainless steel structure
Studio Neda Saeedi

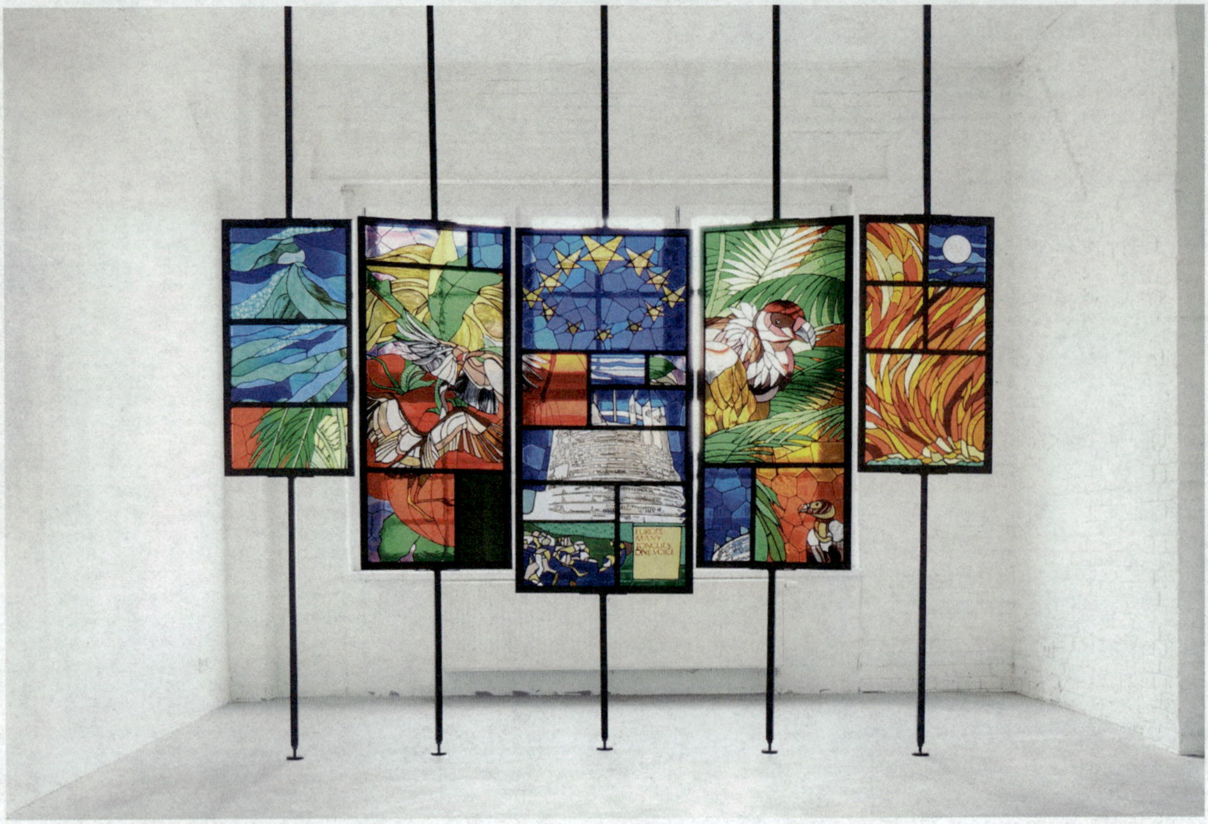

Only Birds Who Fly the Highest Can Stain the Windows, 2022
Stained glass, stainless steel structure
Studio Neda Saeedi

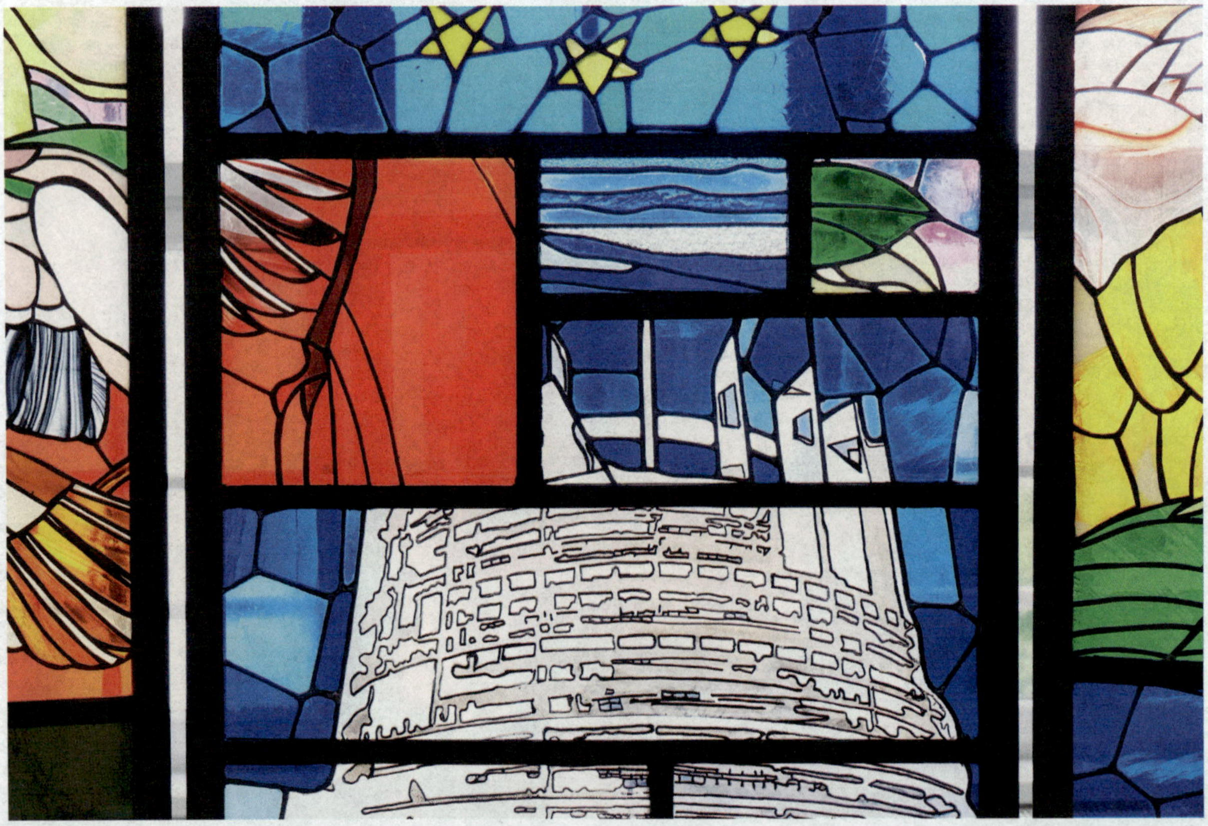

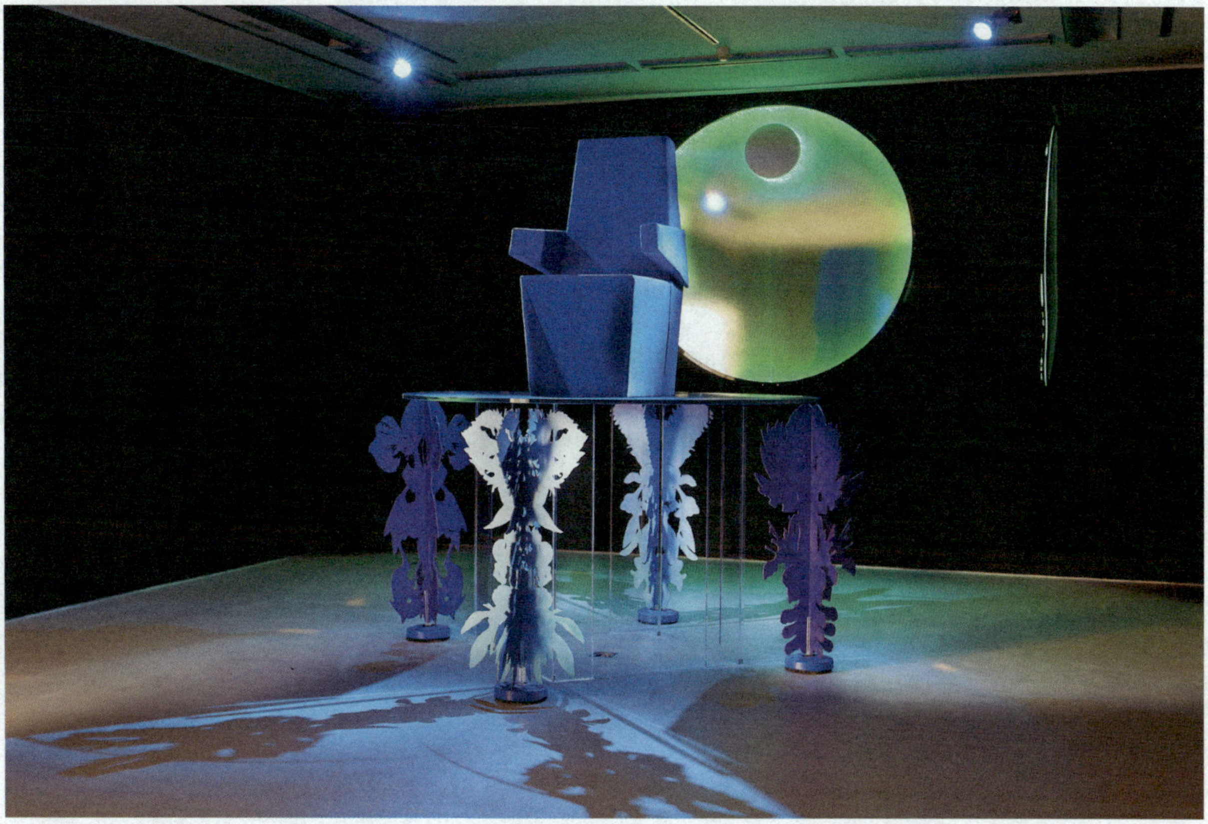

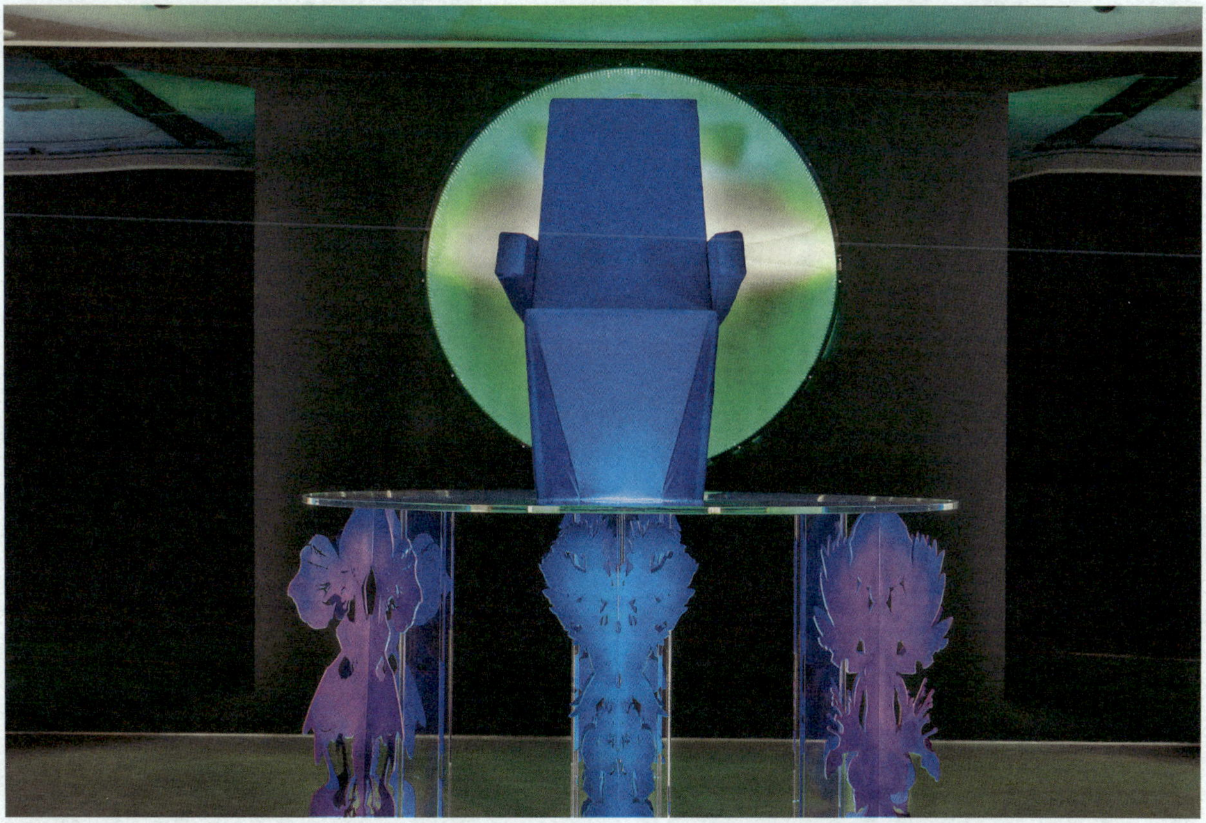

Eziekel Dreams Beyond Repair, 2021
Multimedia installation
Commissioned by Taxispalais Kunsthalle Tirol, Innsbruck, for the exhibition *HEXEN*

Two Shades of Green, 2021
Multimedia installation
Staatliche Kunsthalle Baden-Baden
Argo Factory, Pejman Foundation, Tehran

Two Shades of Green, 2021
Multimedia installation
Staatliche Kunsthalle Baden-Baden
Argo Factory, Pejman Foundation, Tehran

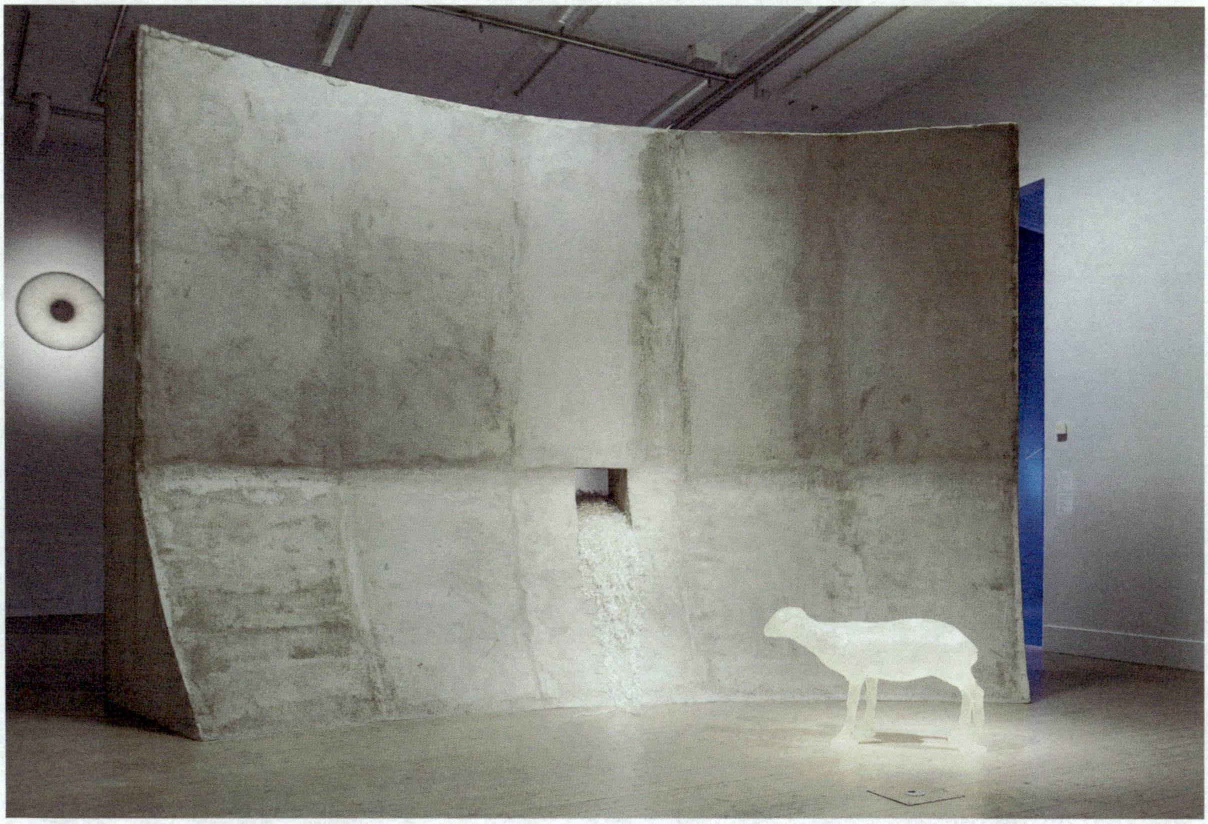

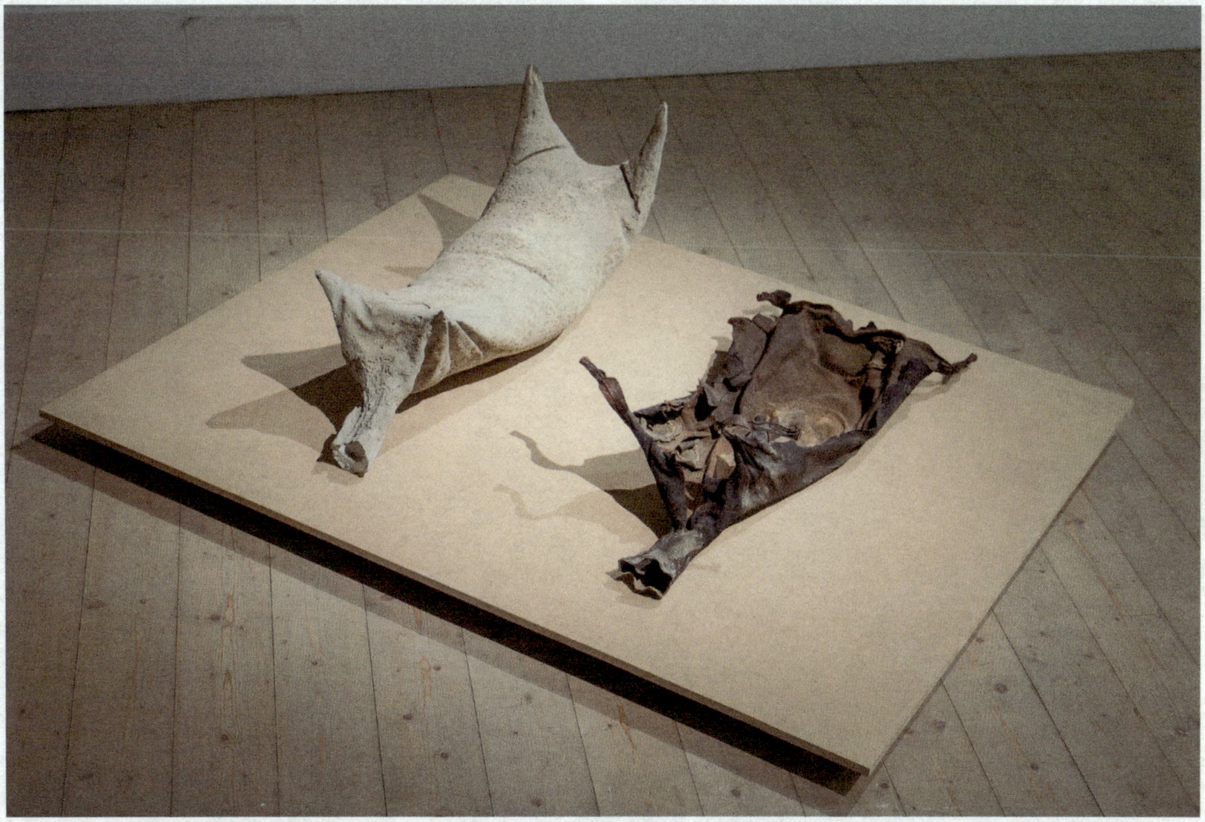

Garden of Eden Moving; A Petrified Tribe, 2018 / 2019
Multimedia installation
Luleå Biennial 2018, Sweden
Dastan Basement Gallery, Tehran

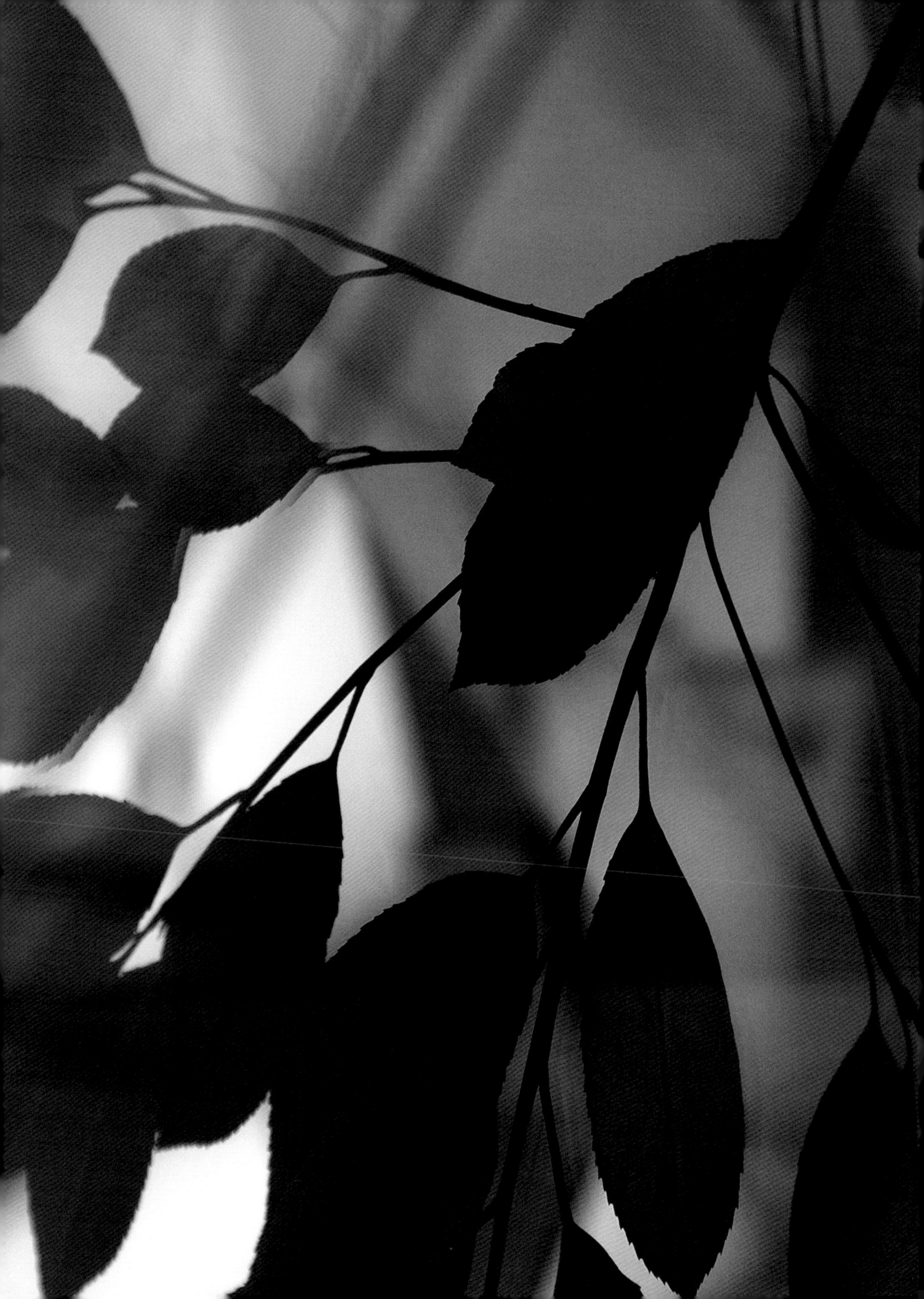

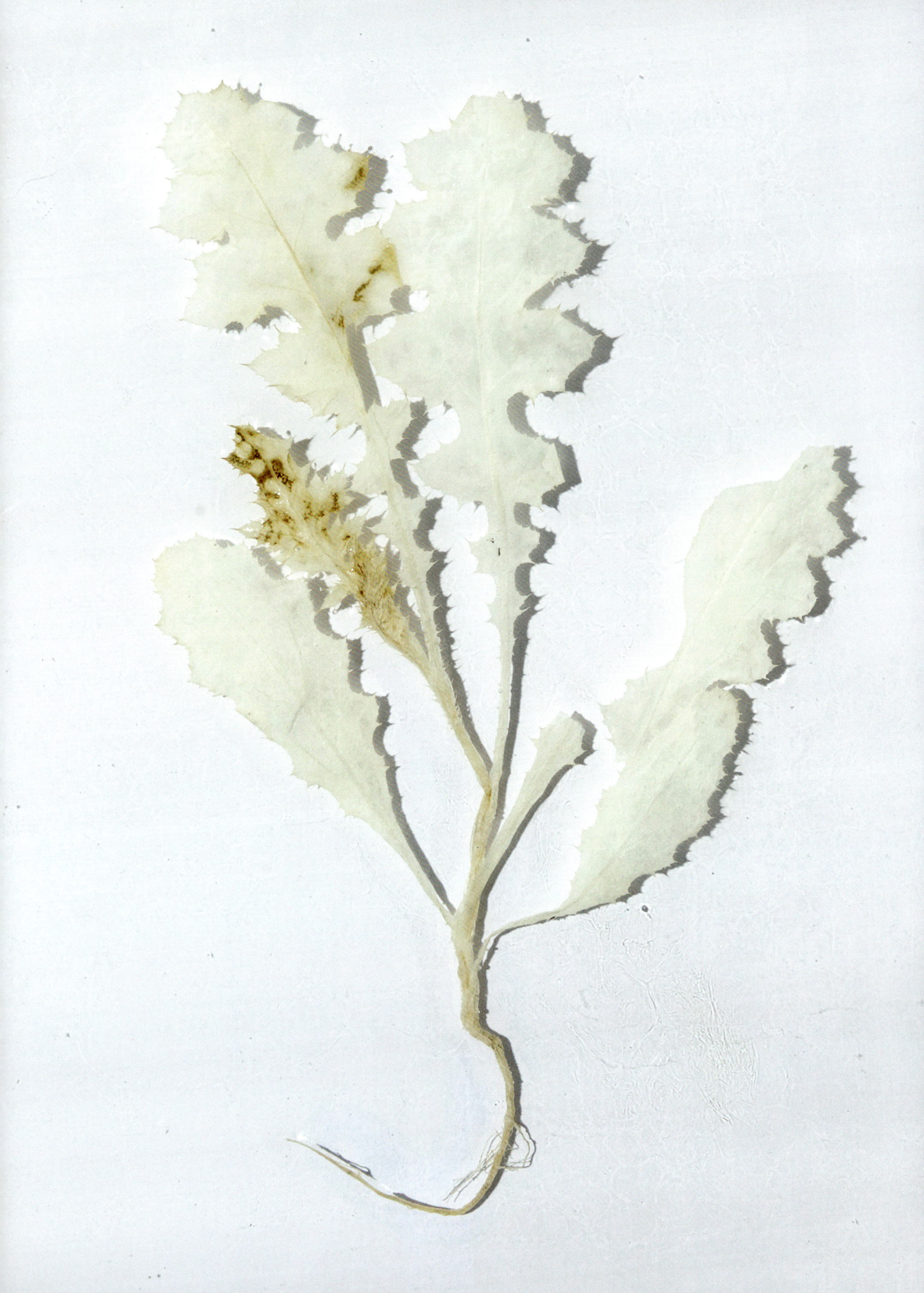

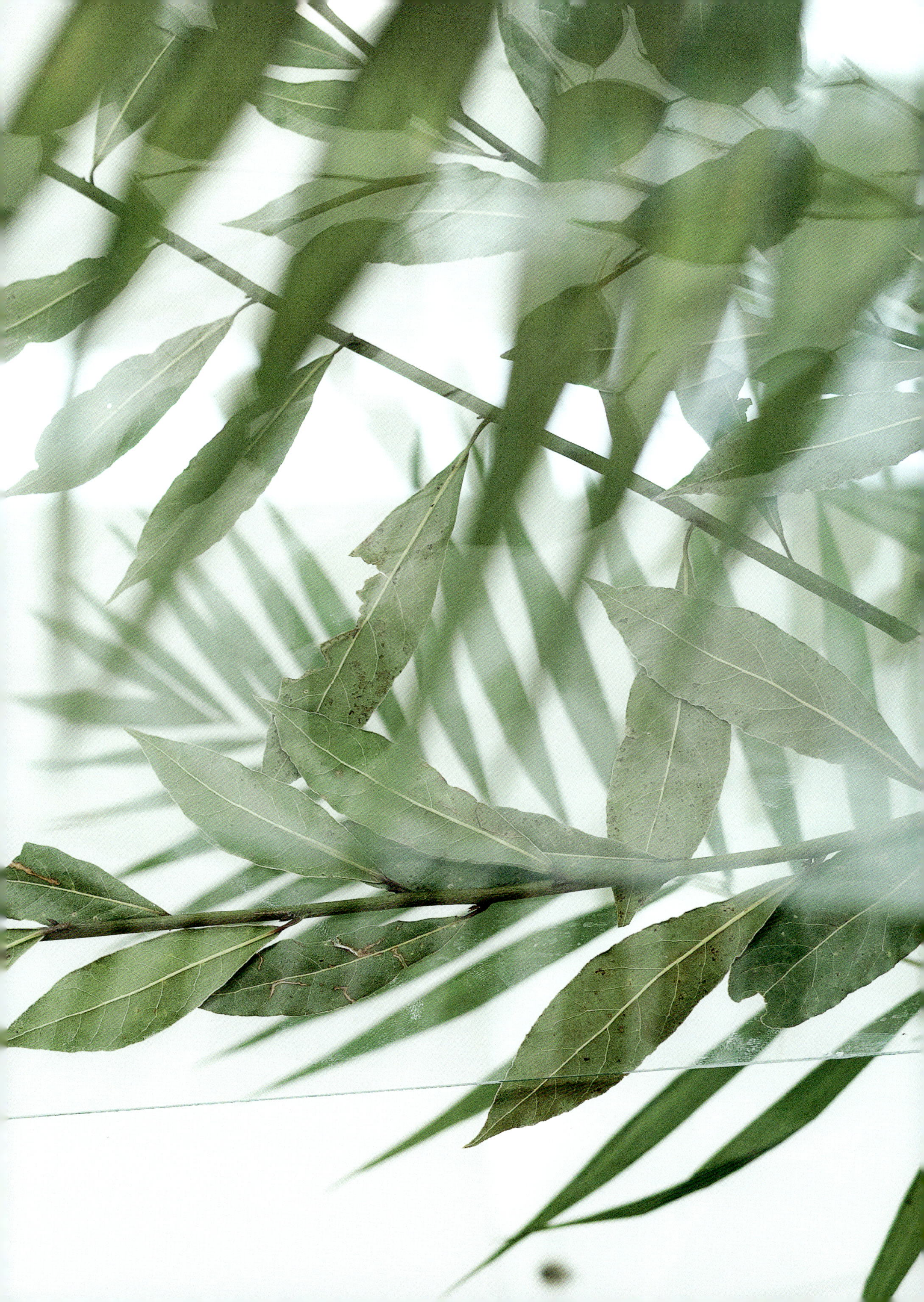

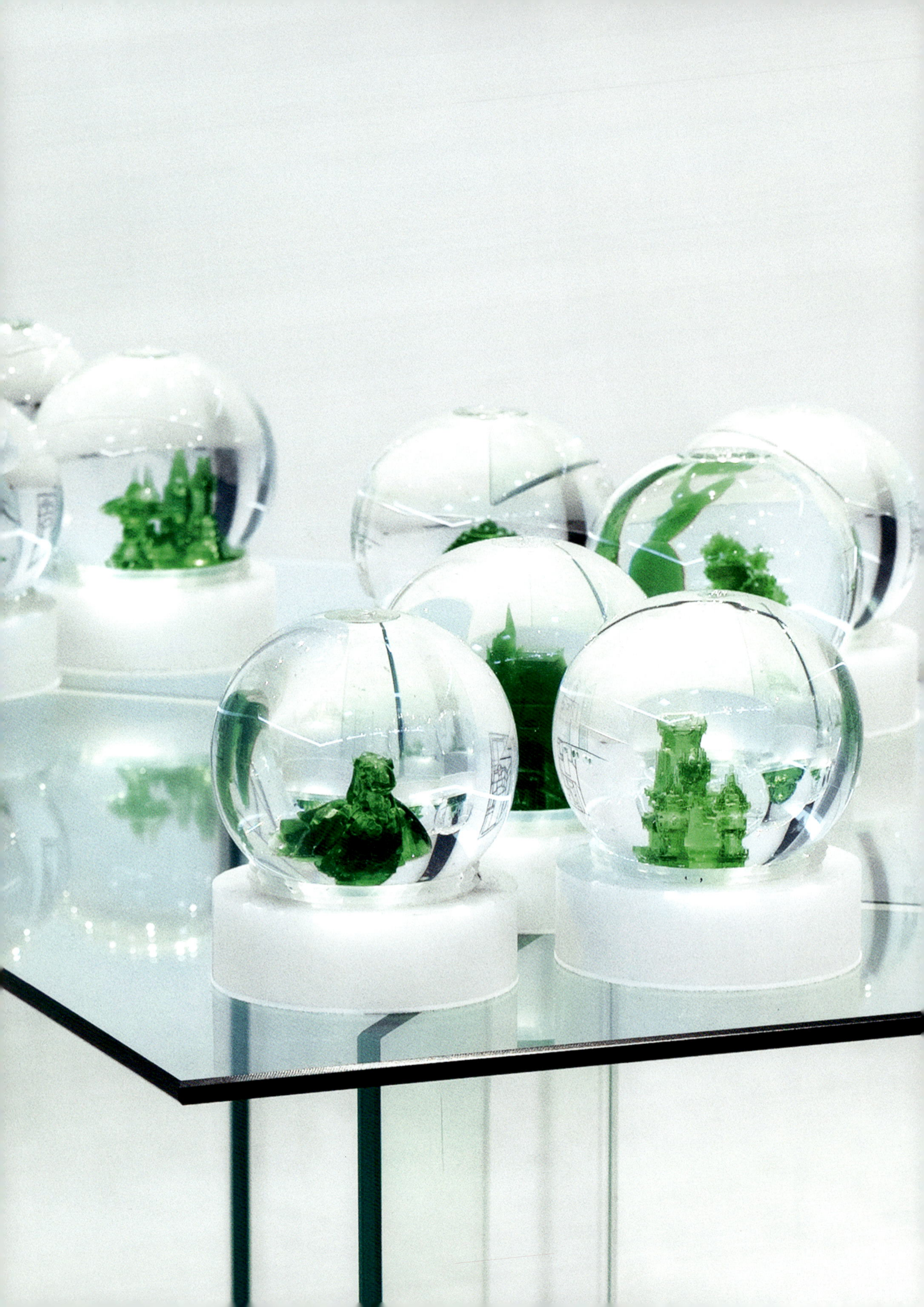

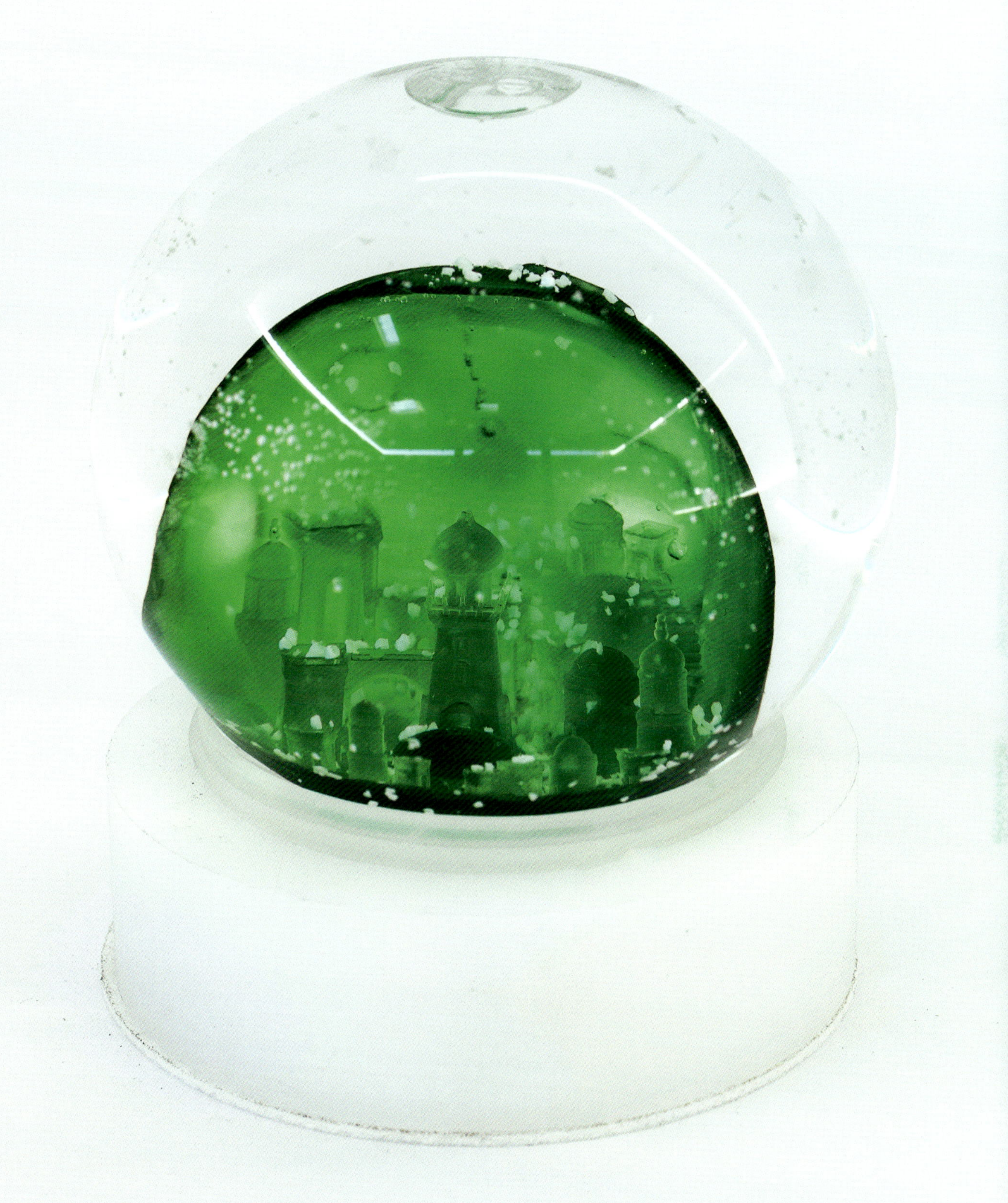

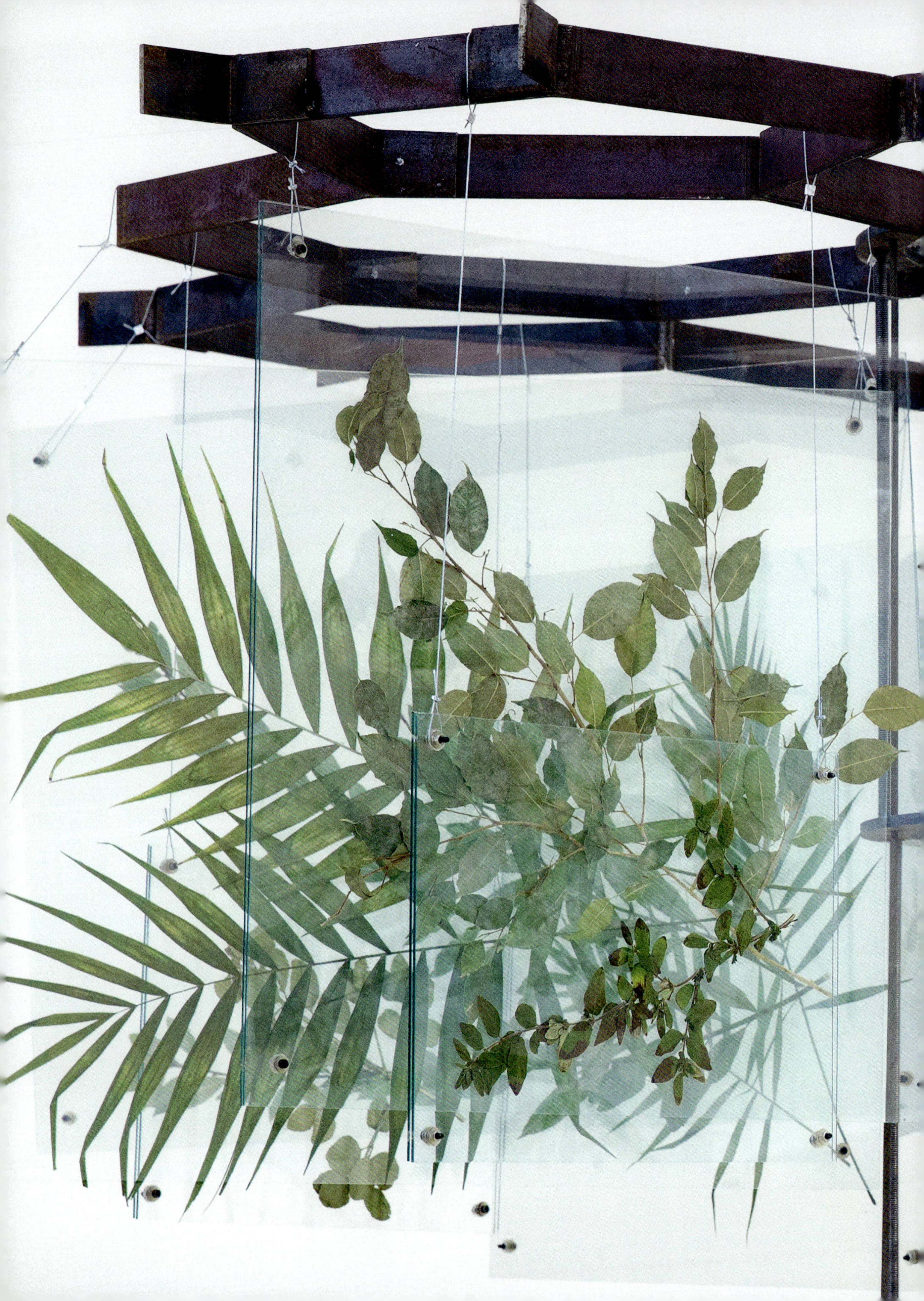

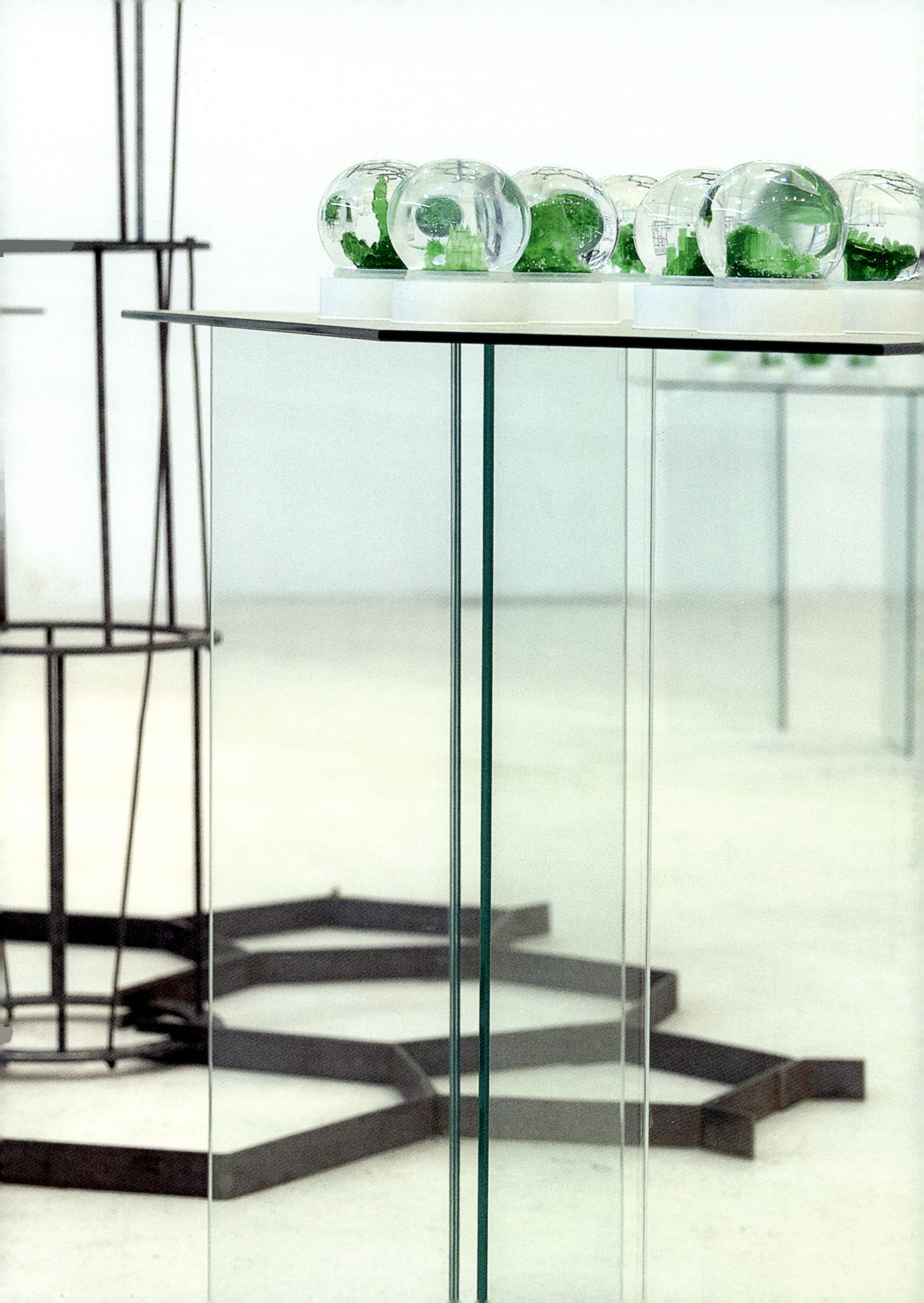

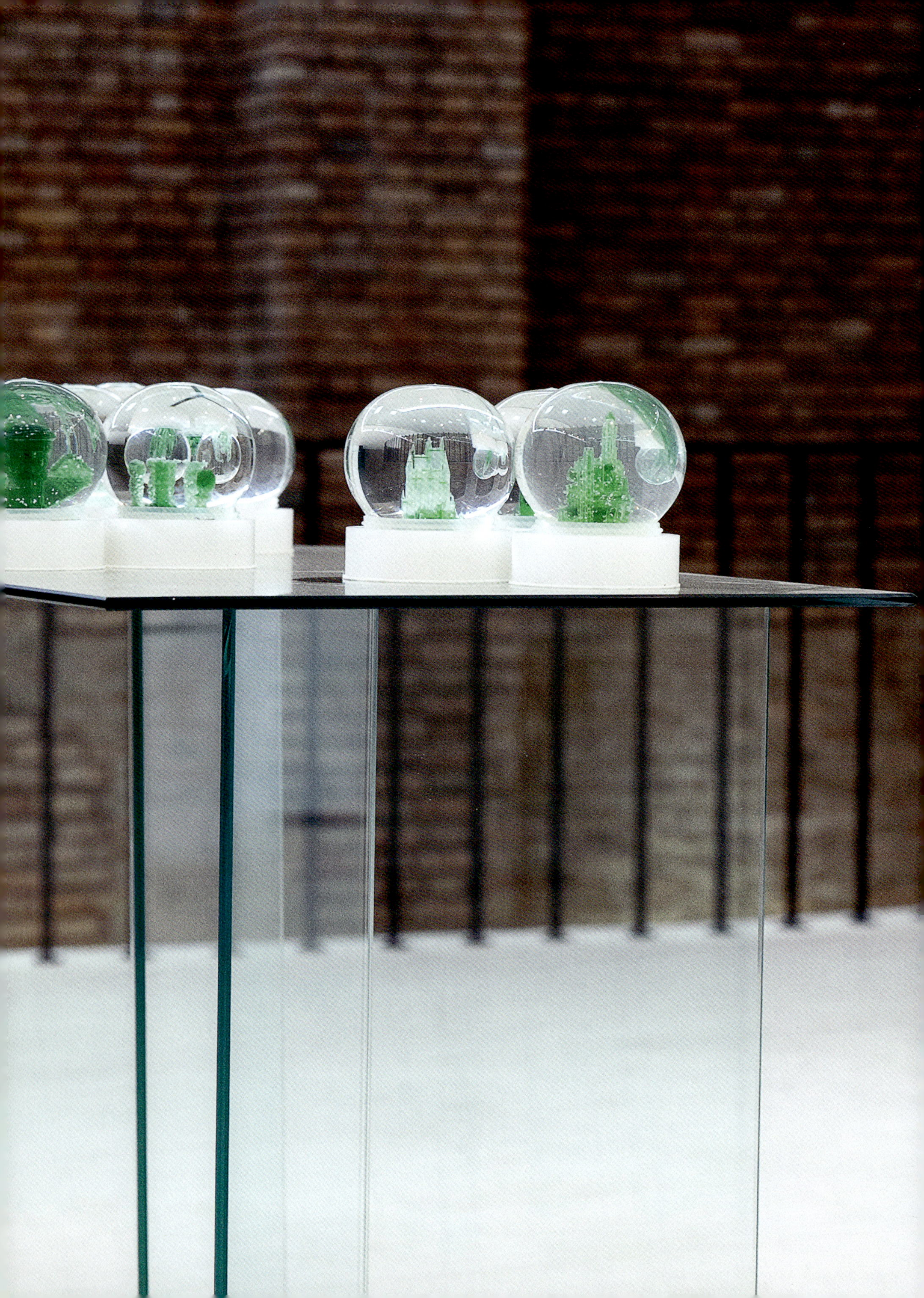

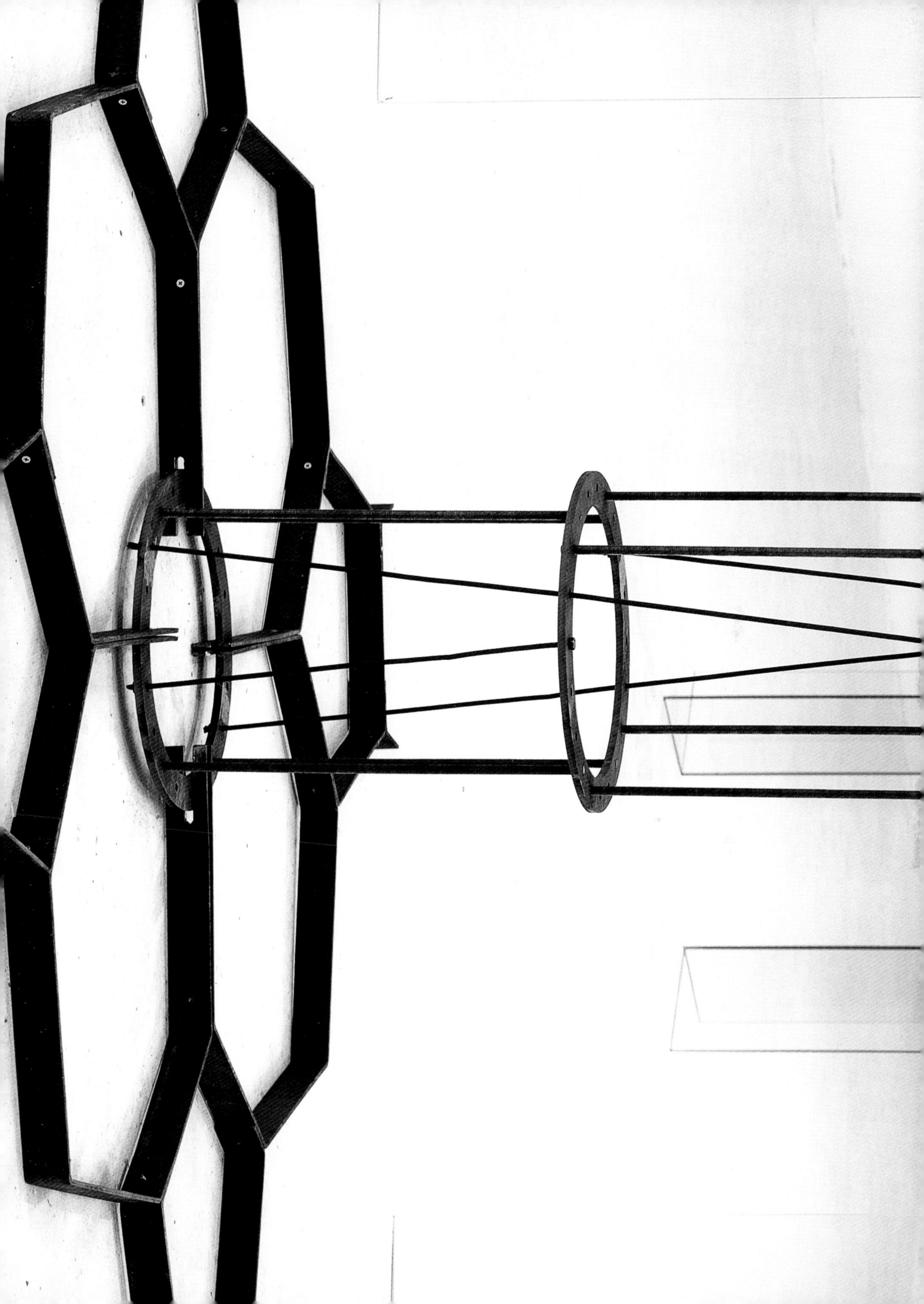

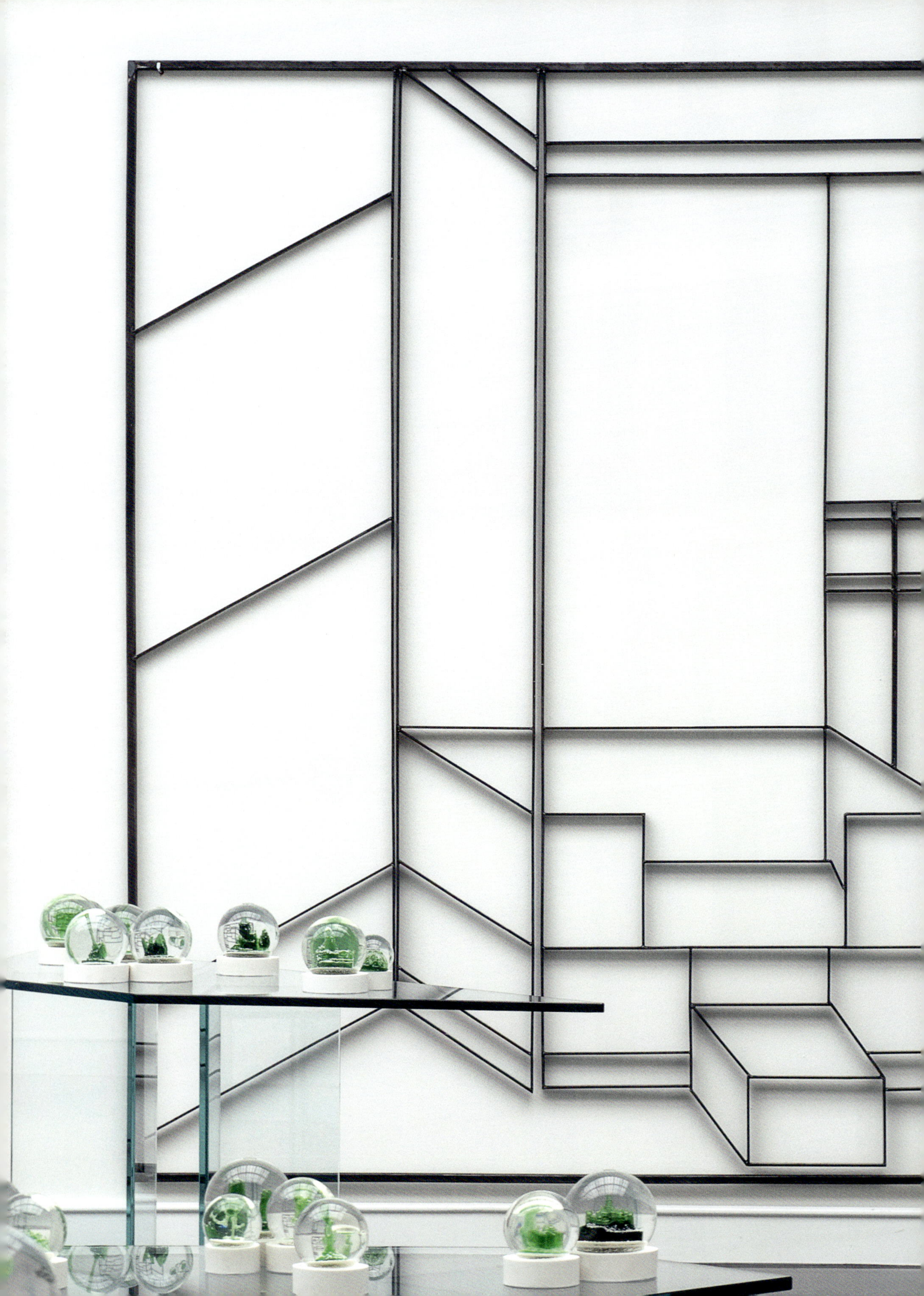

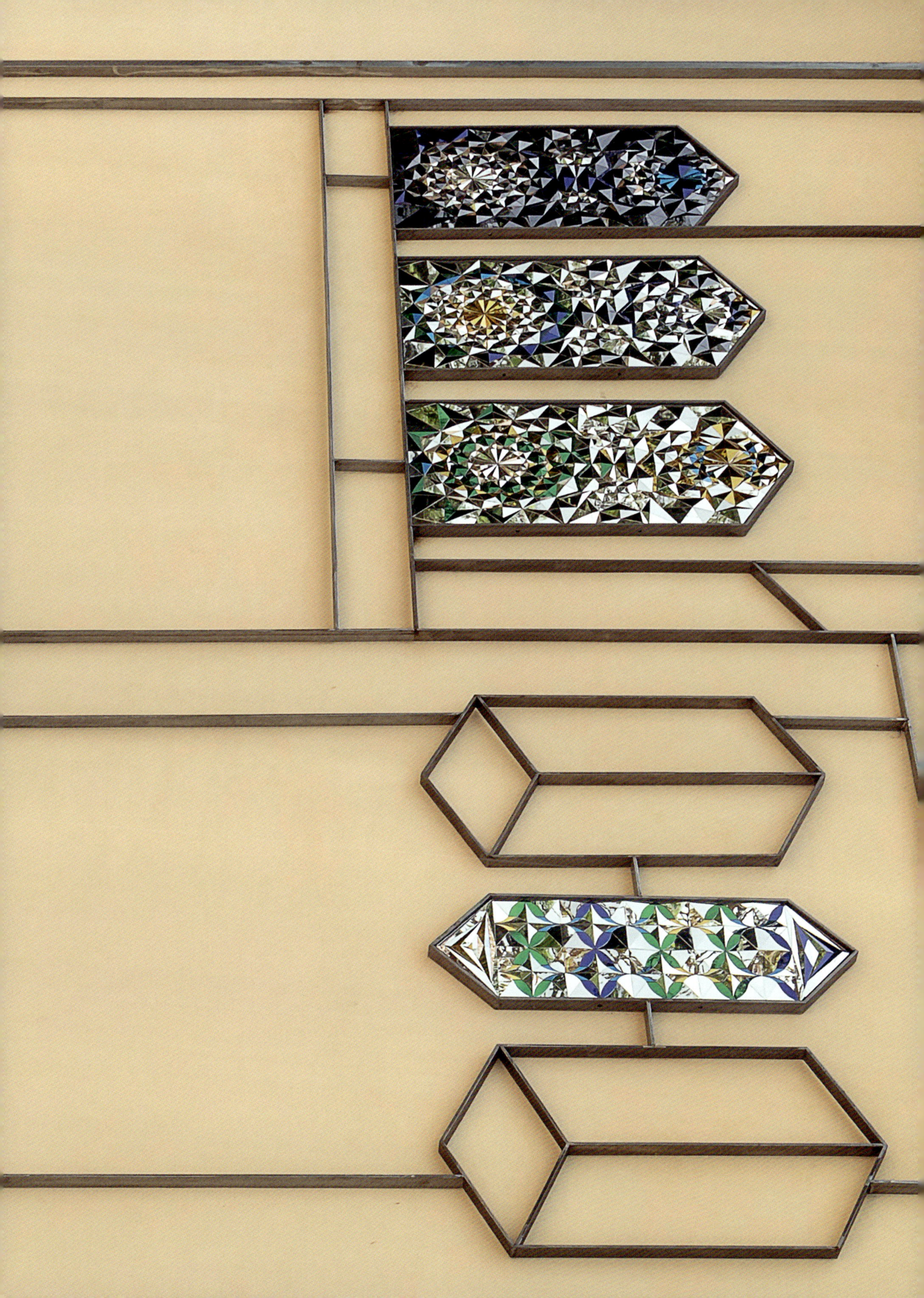

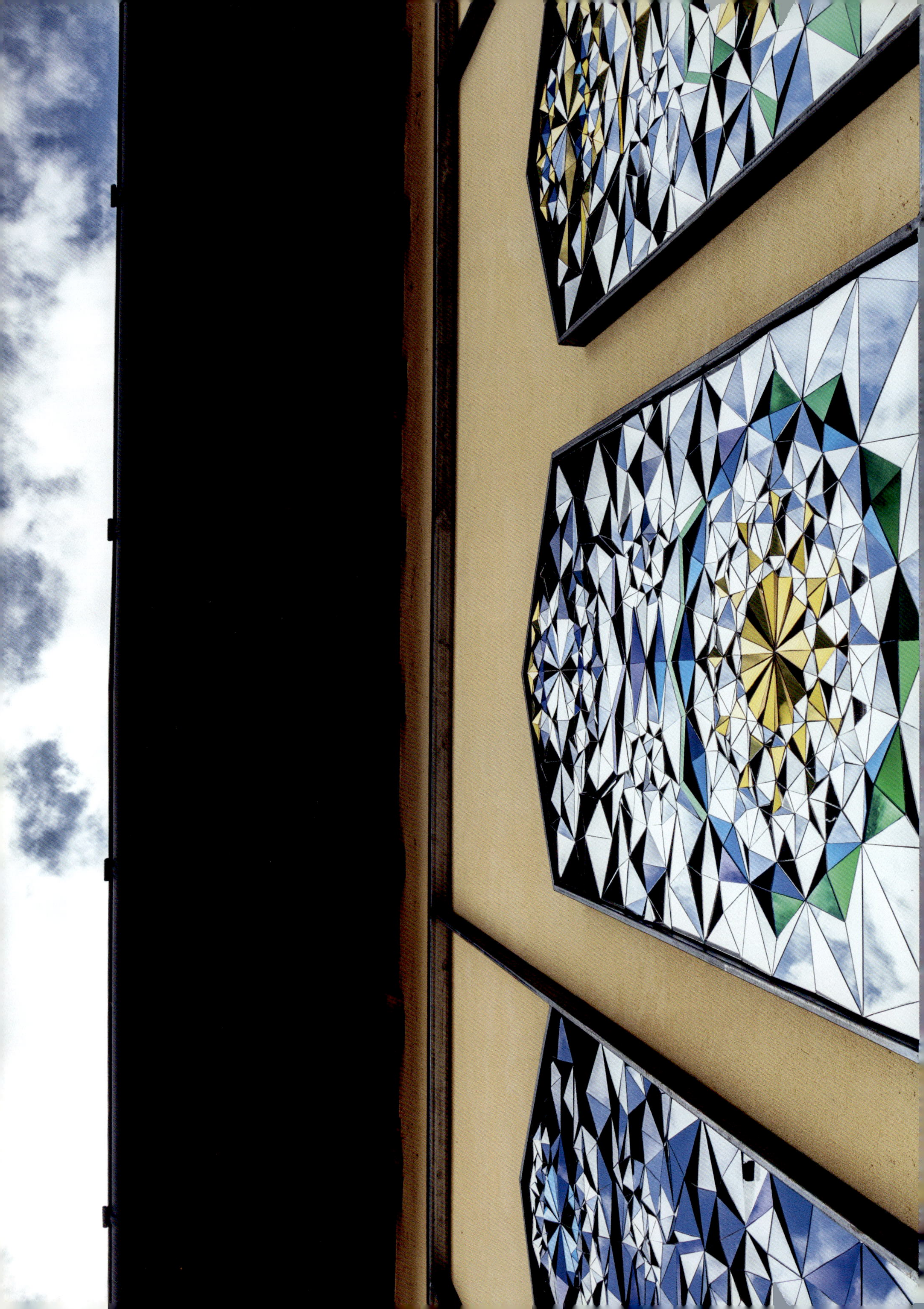

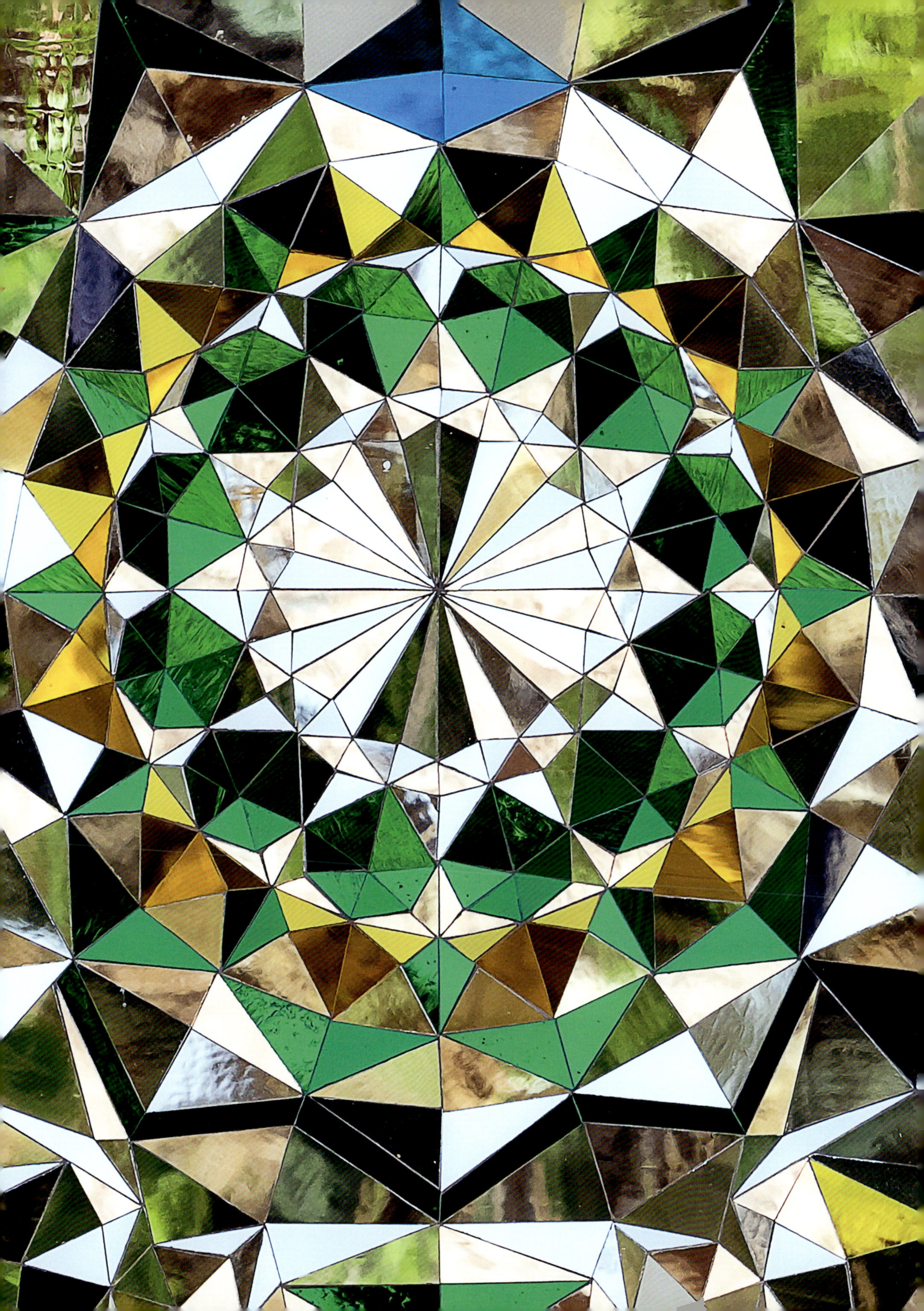

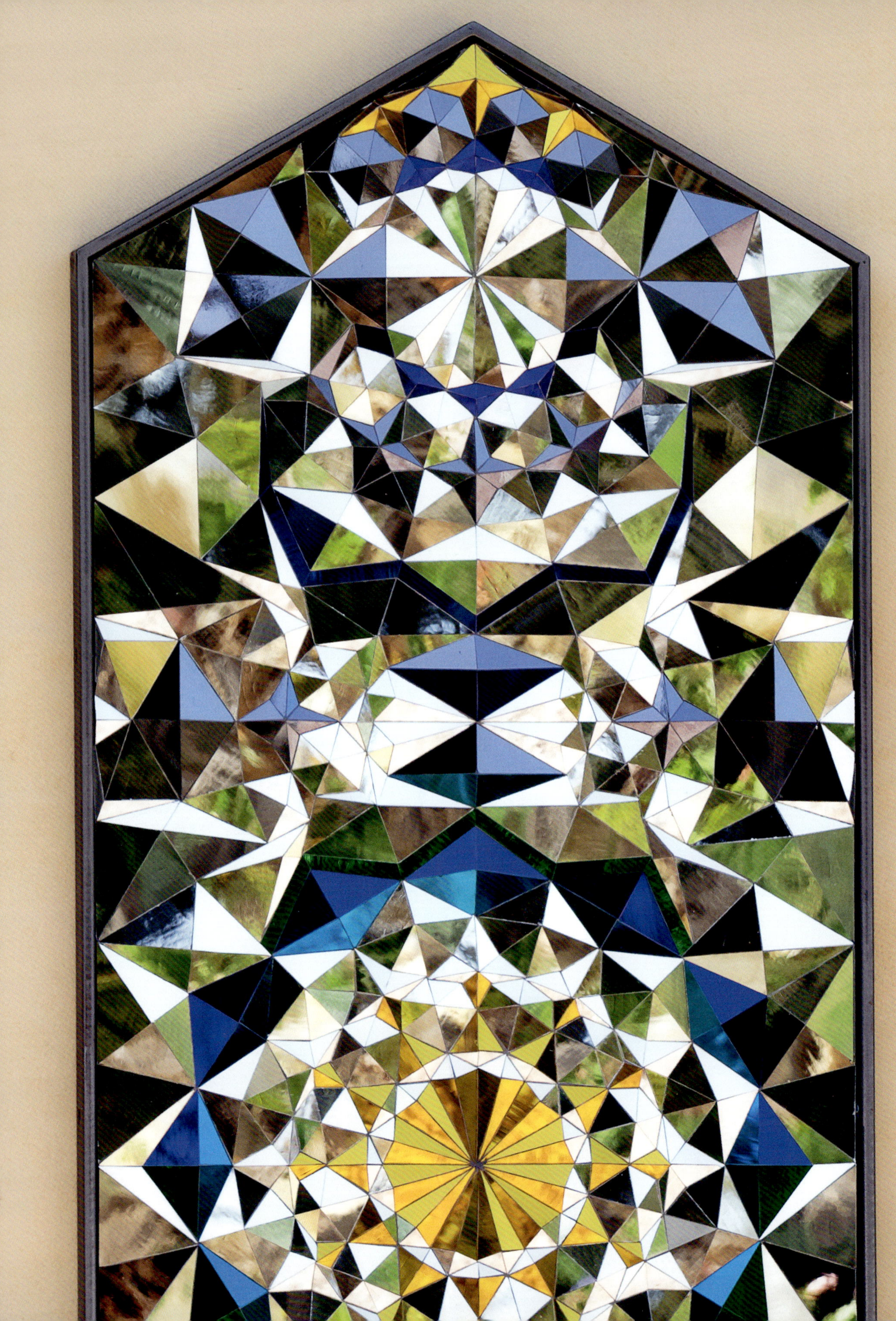

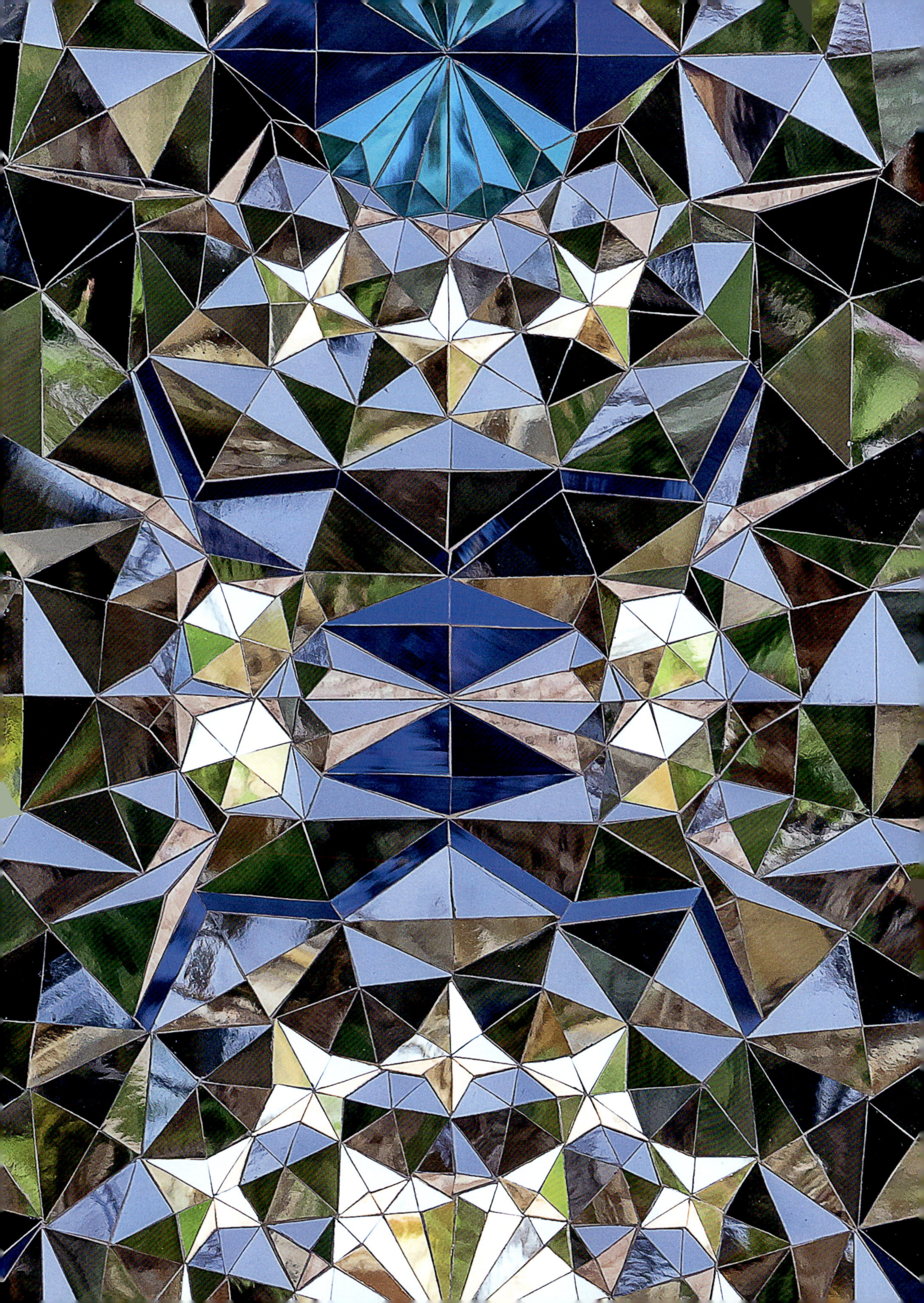

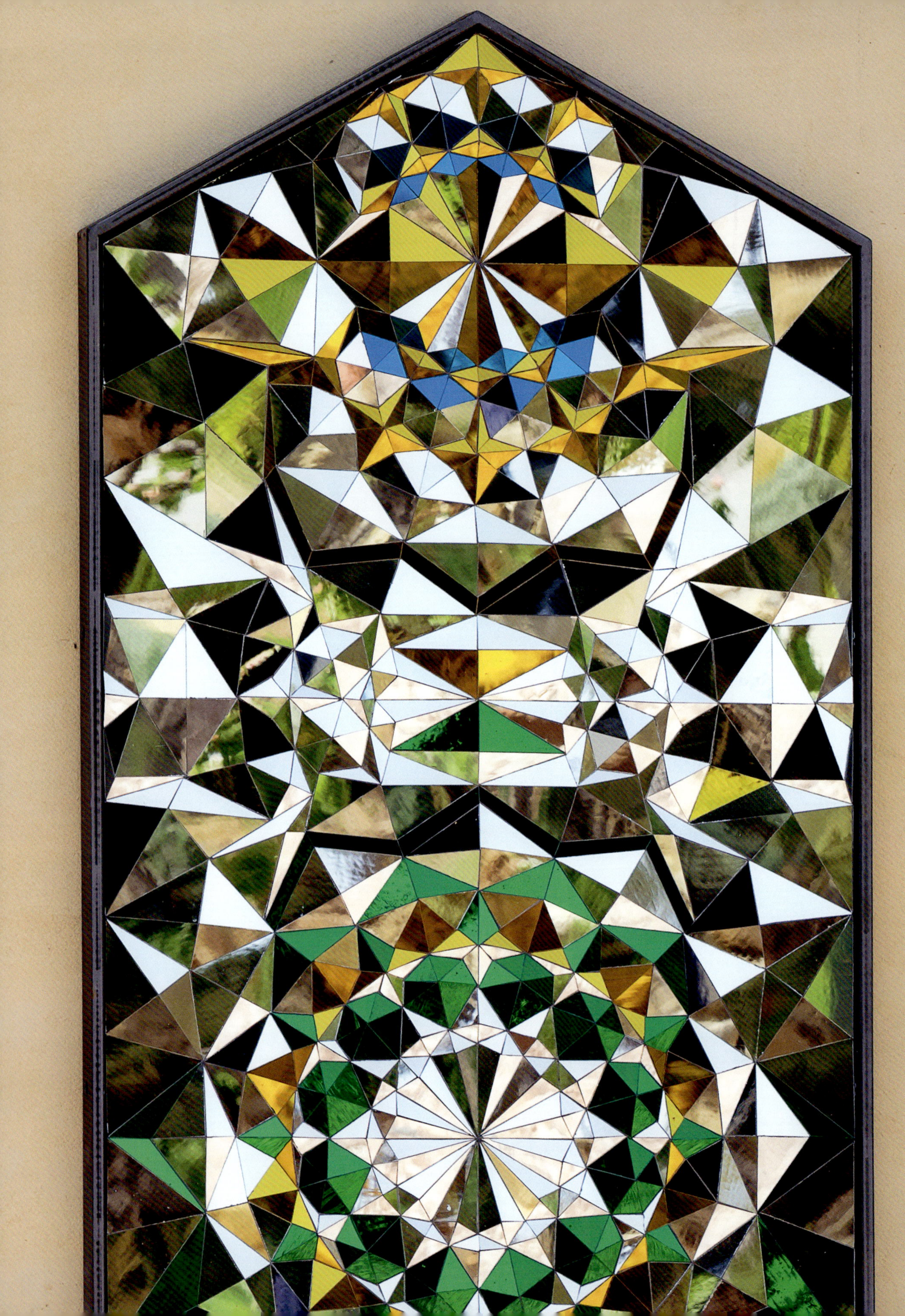

I was working a lot with the metaphor
and notion of the garden in a sense
of something that has a binary system.
Between nature and culture. In my
opinion, we always have this binary zero–
one system, which can be traced back to
religion. There's always the act
of segregation and evaluation.

Sometimes I talk about a specific place
and other times I talk about gardens
as such.

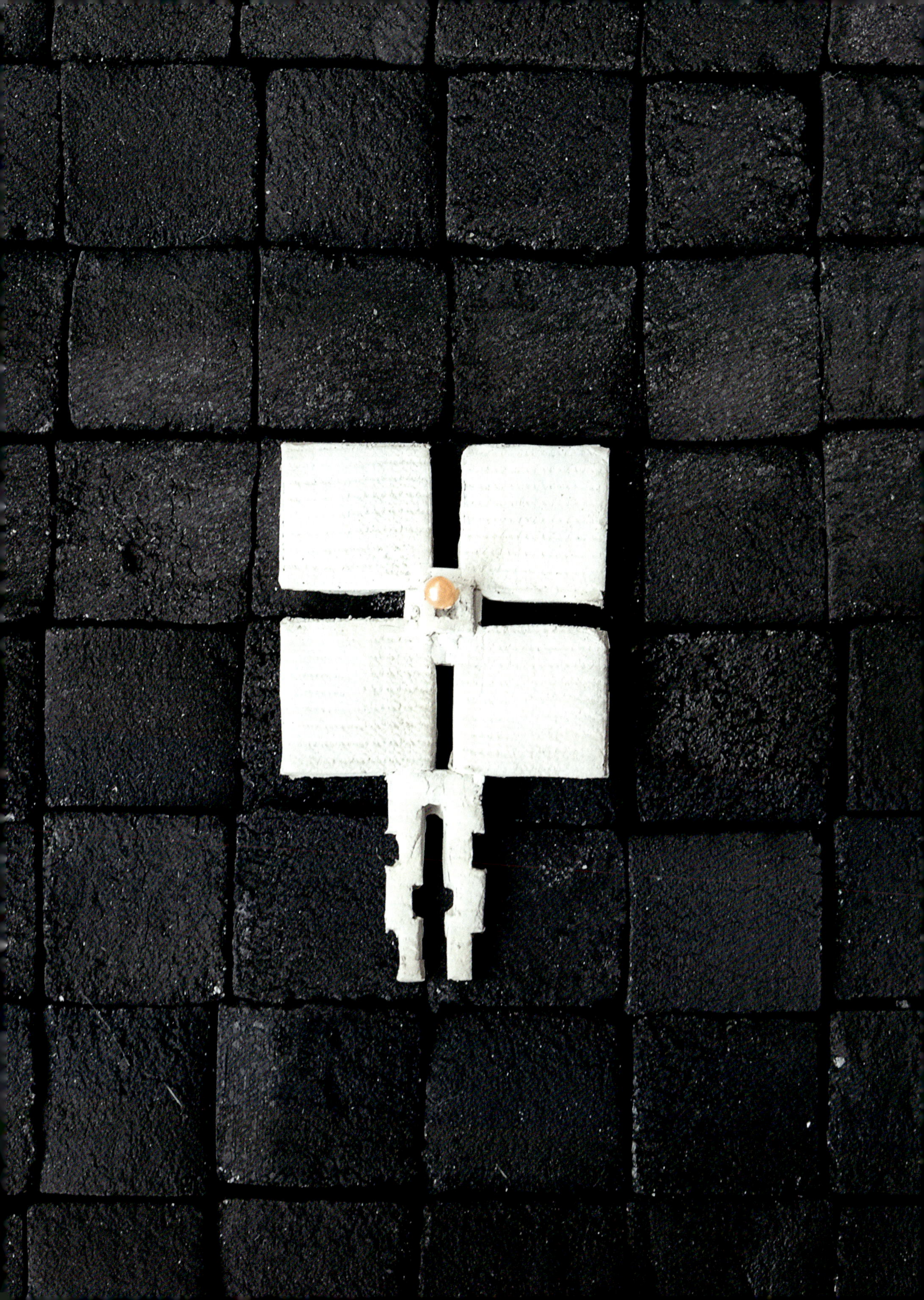

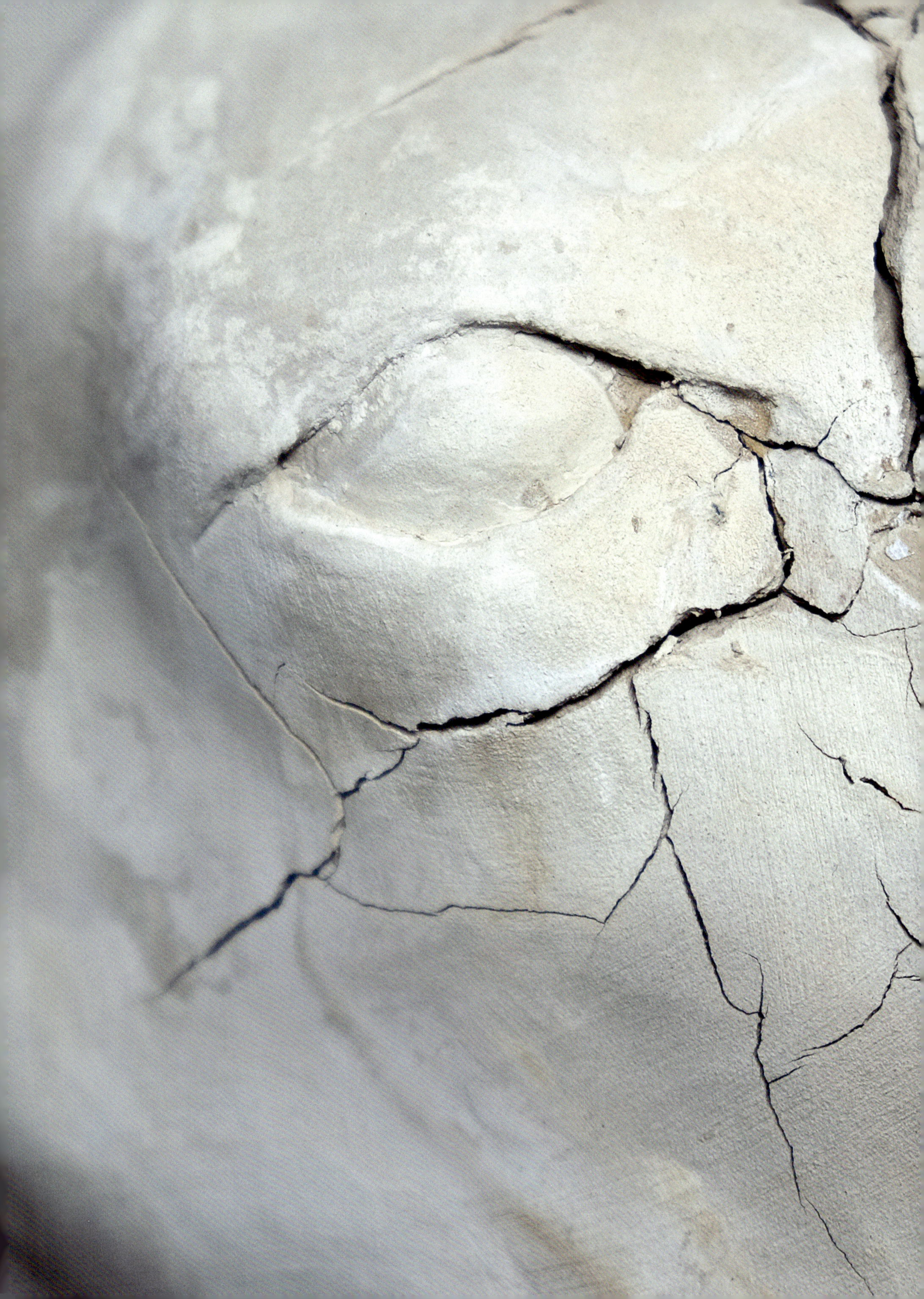

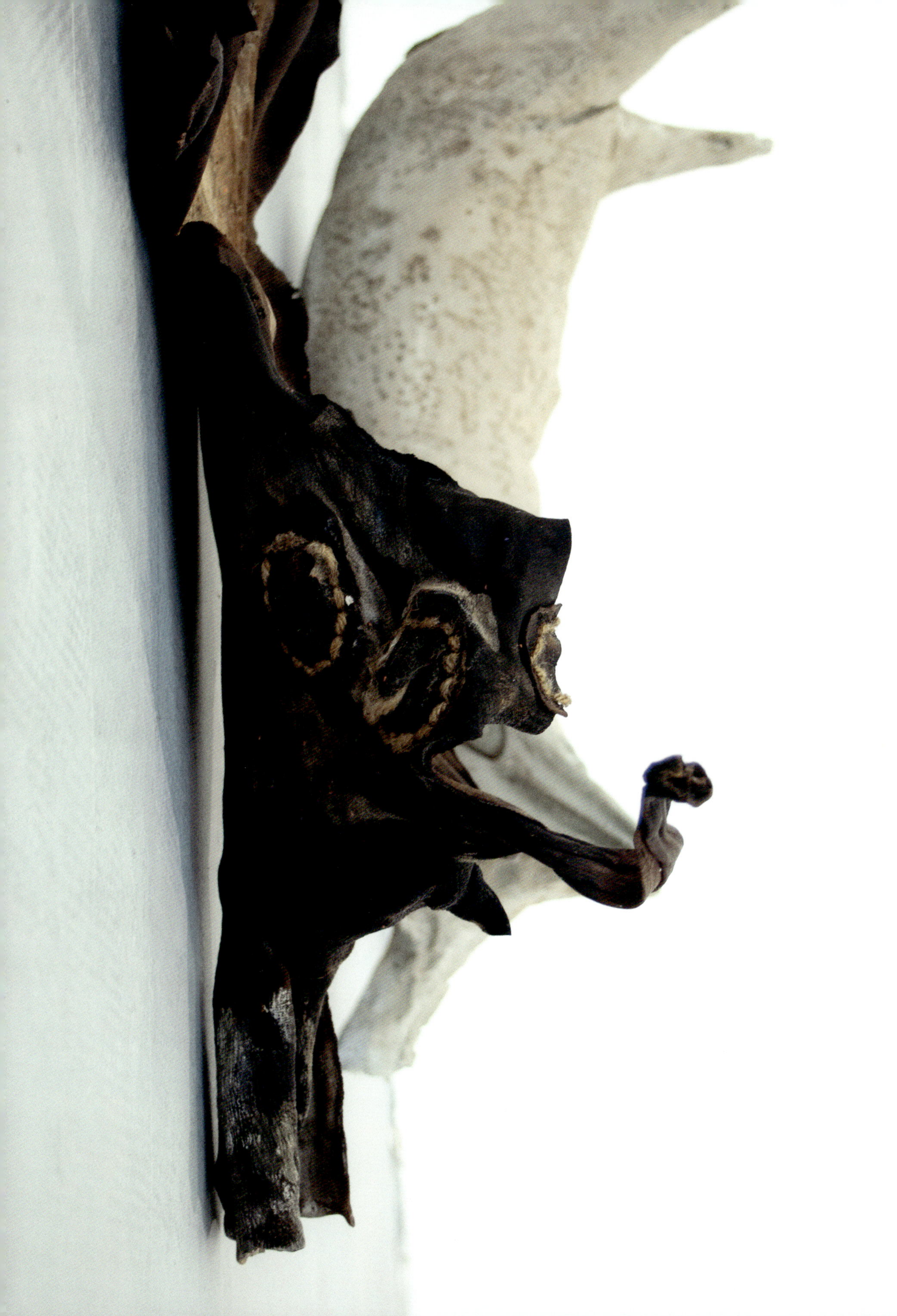

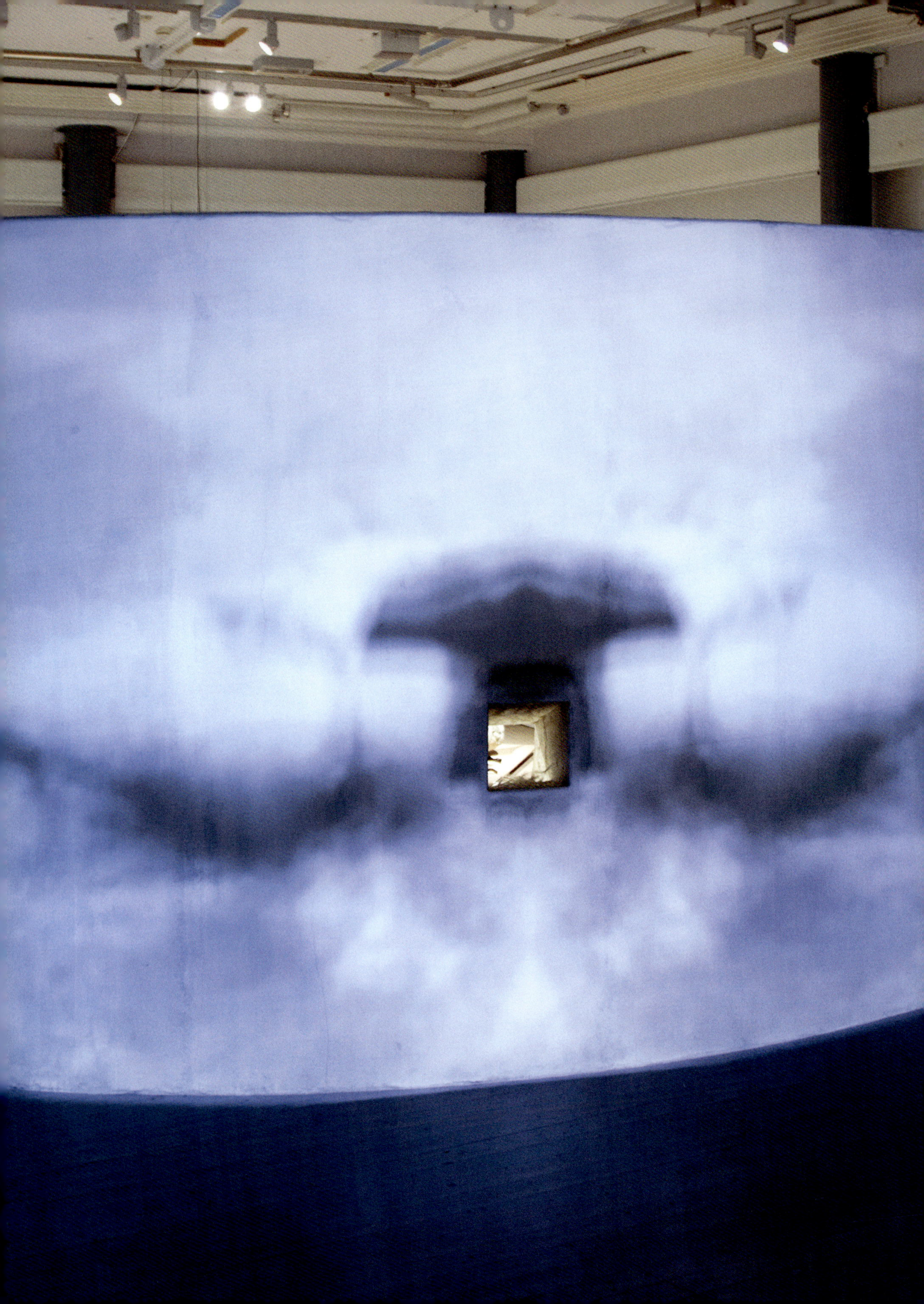

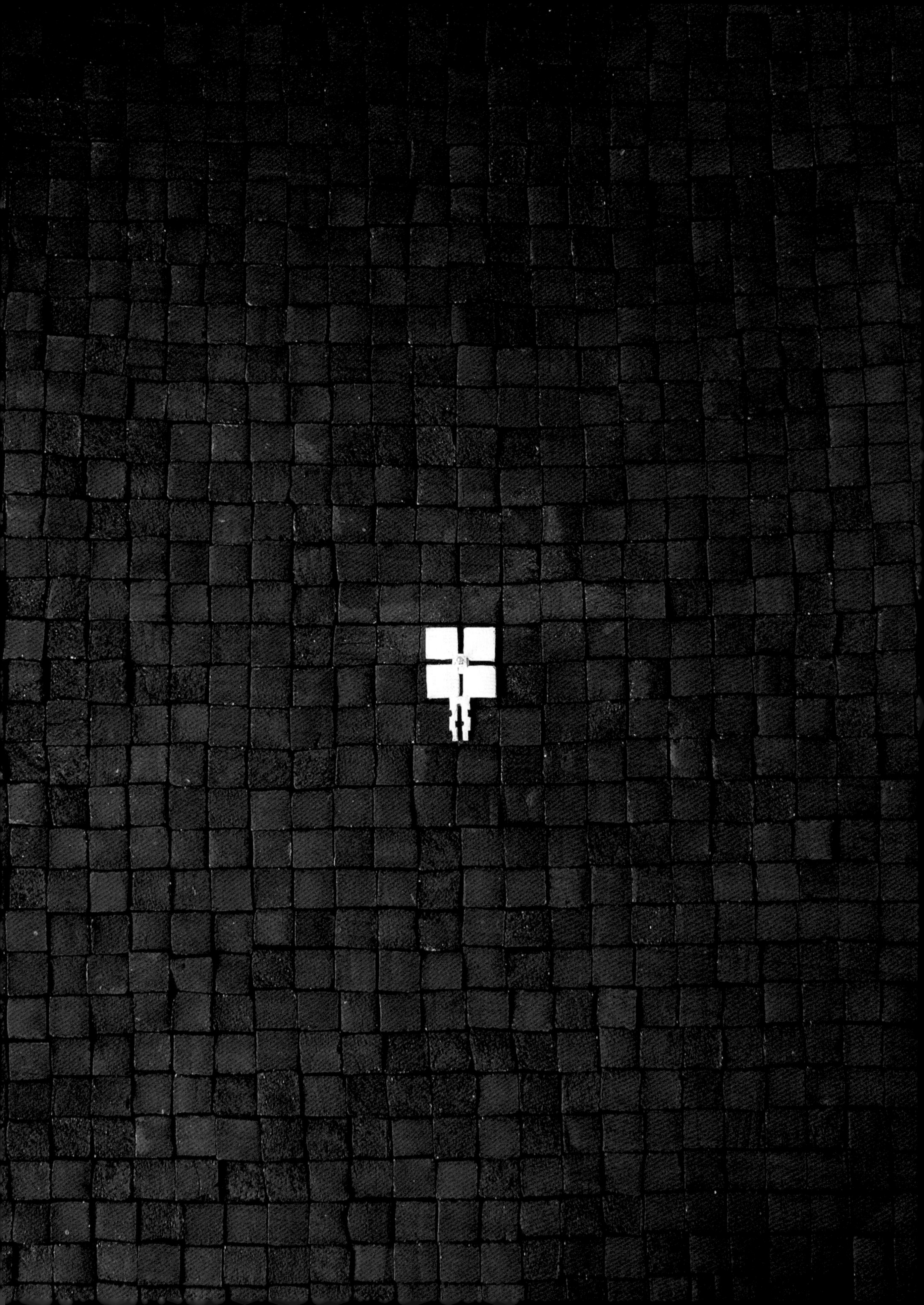

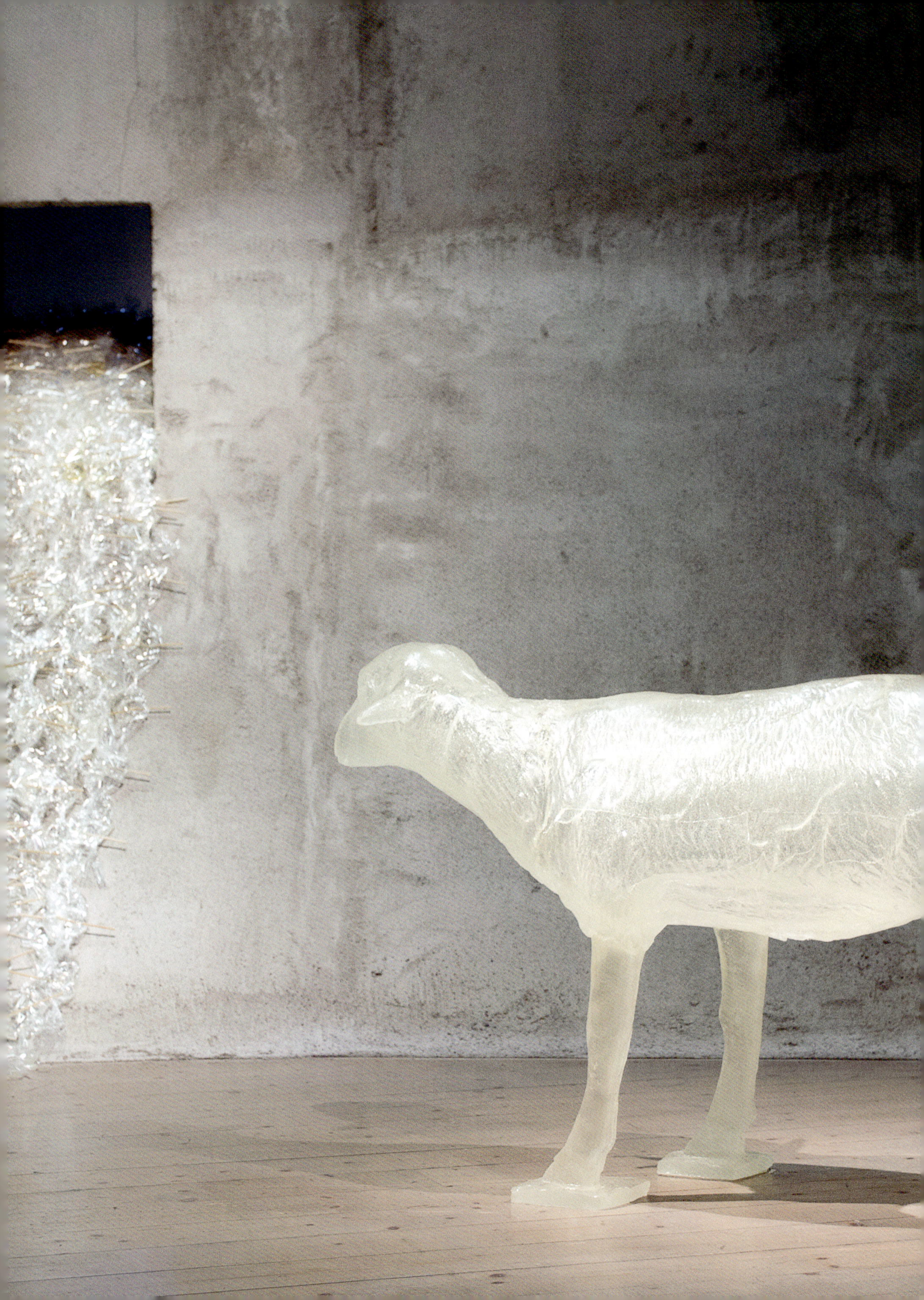

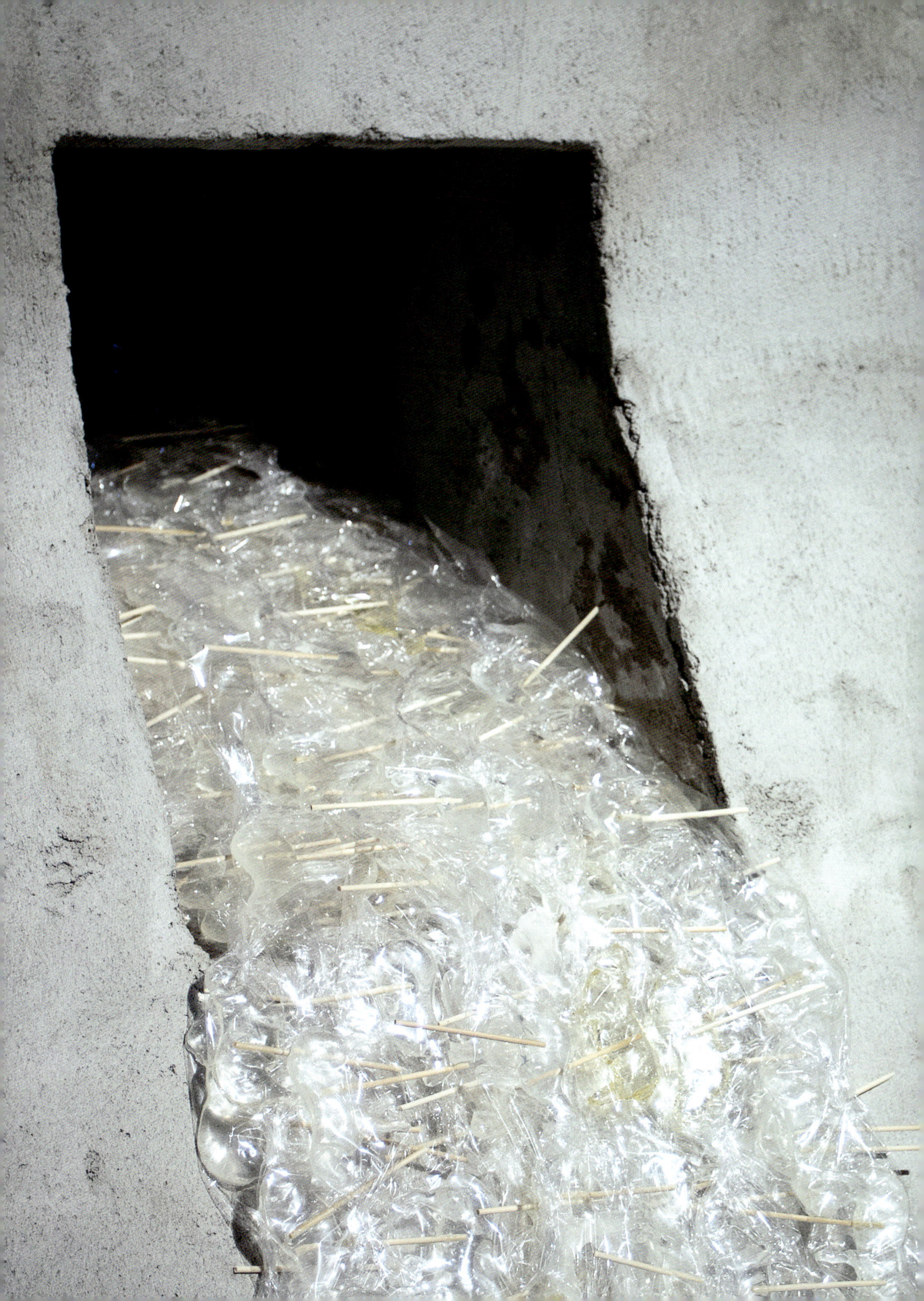

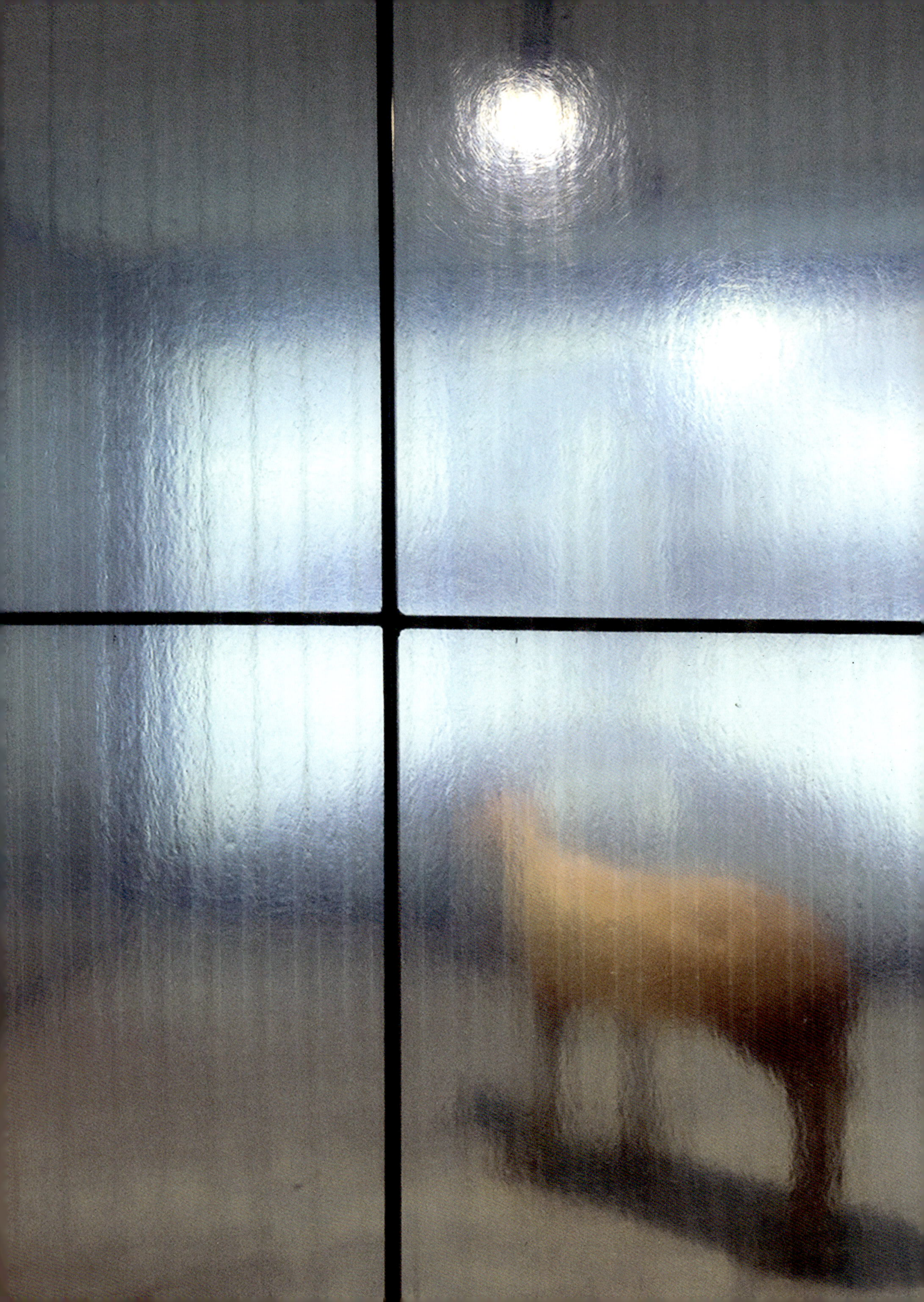

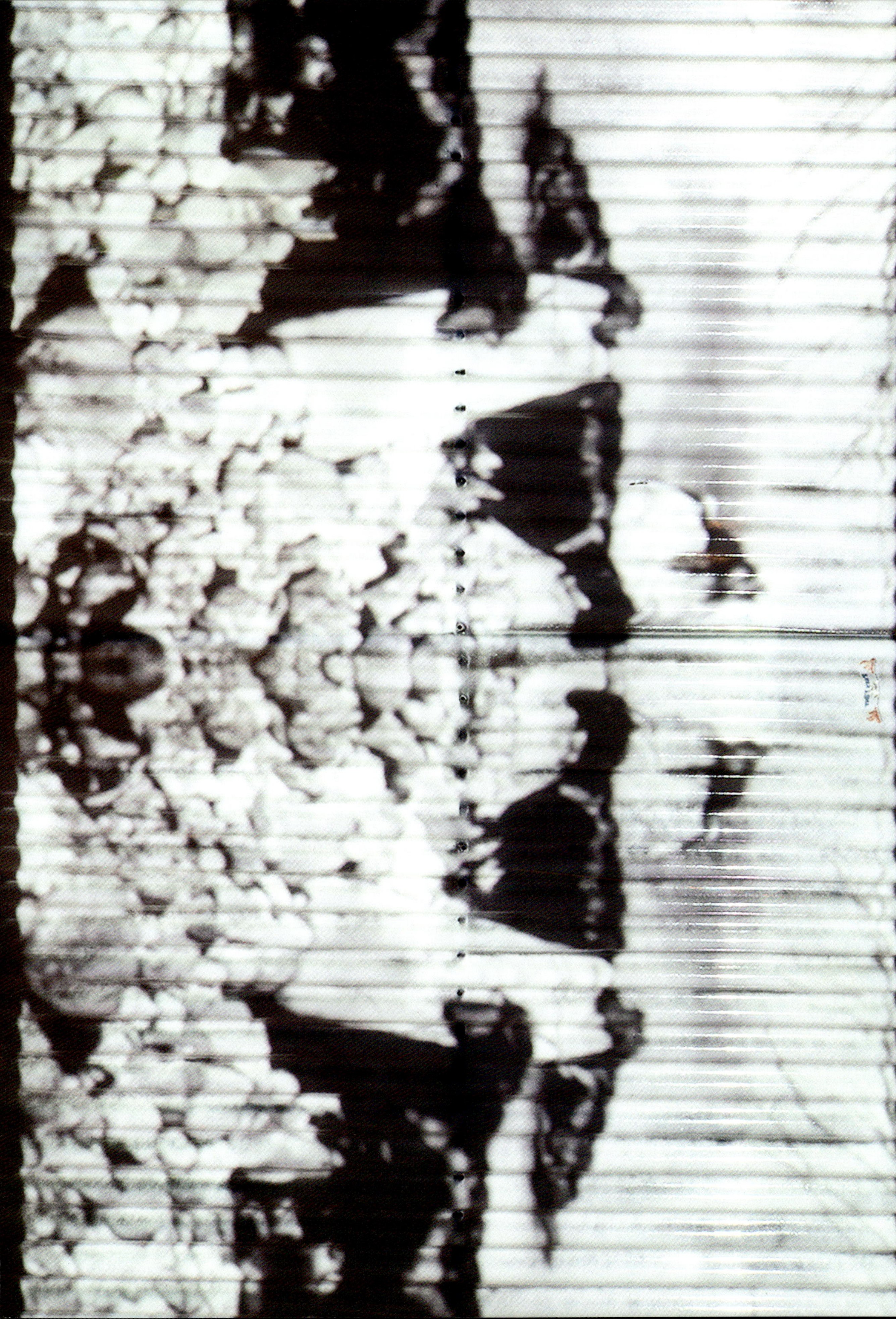

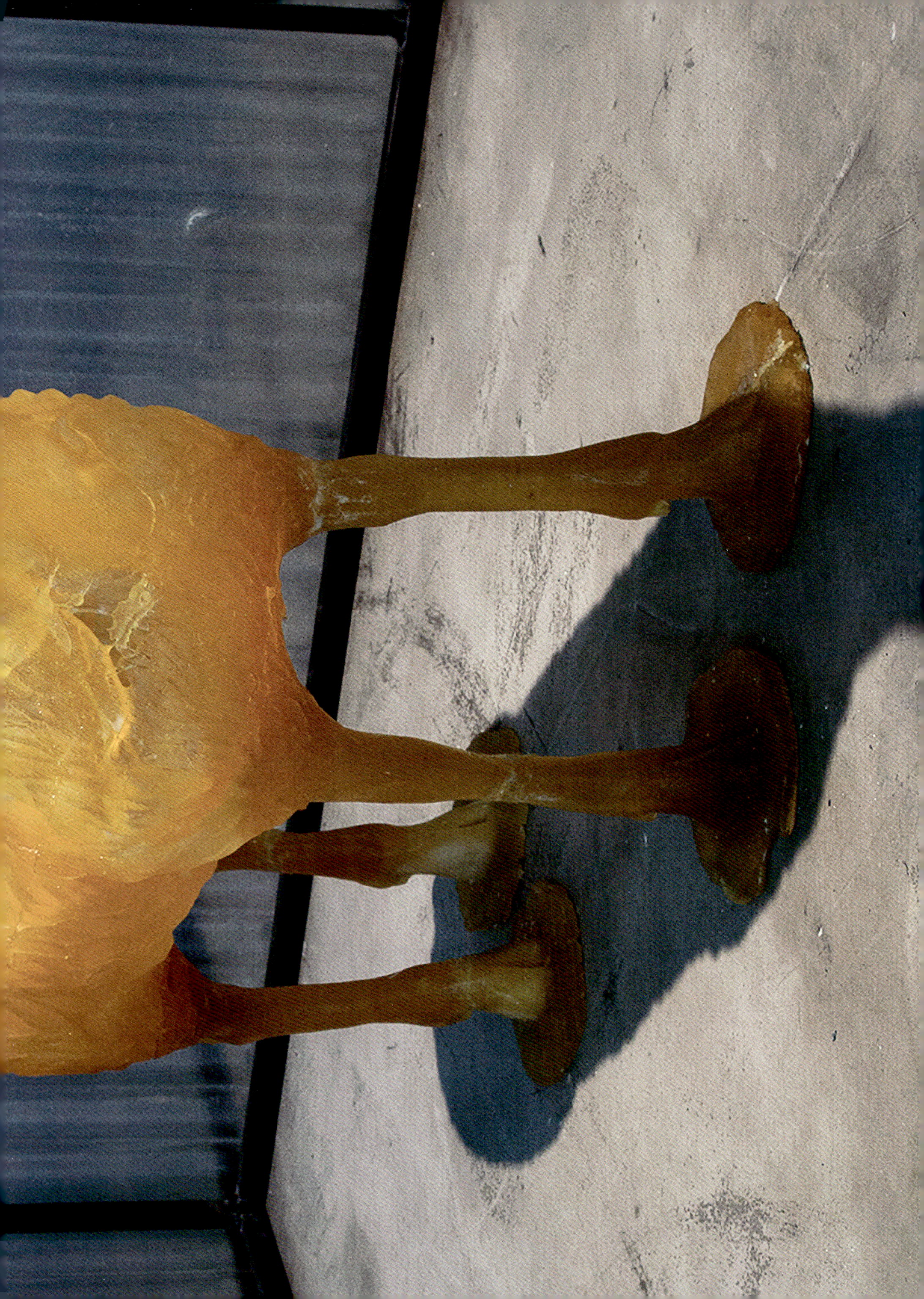

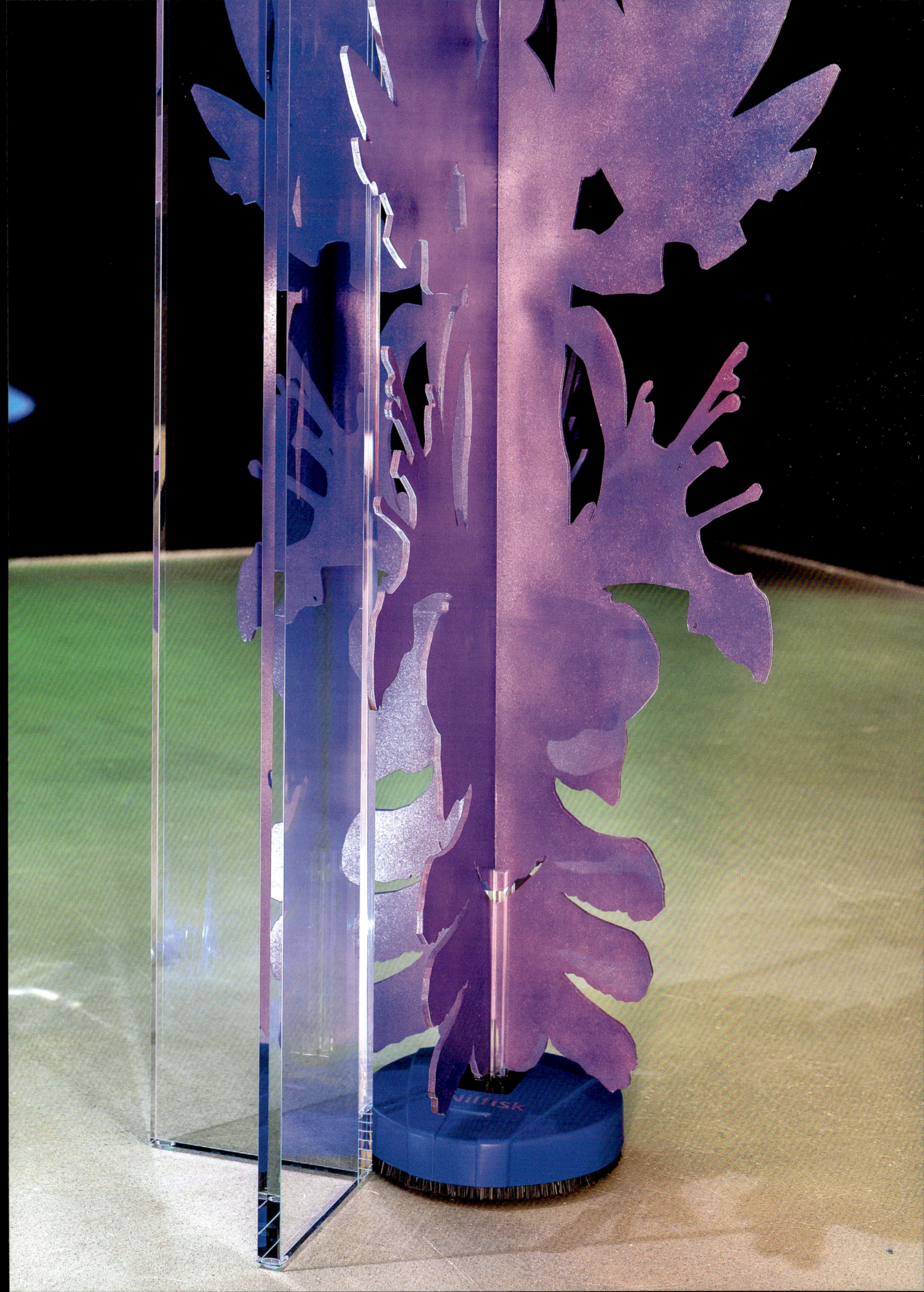

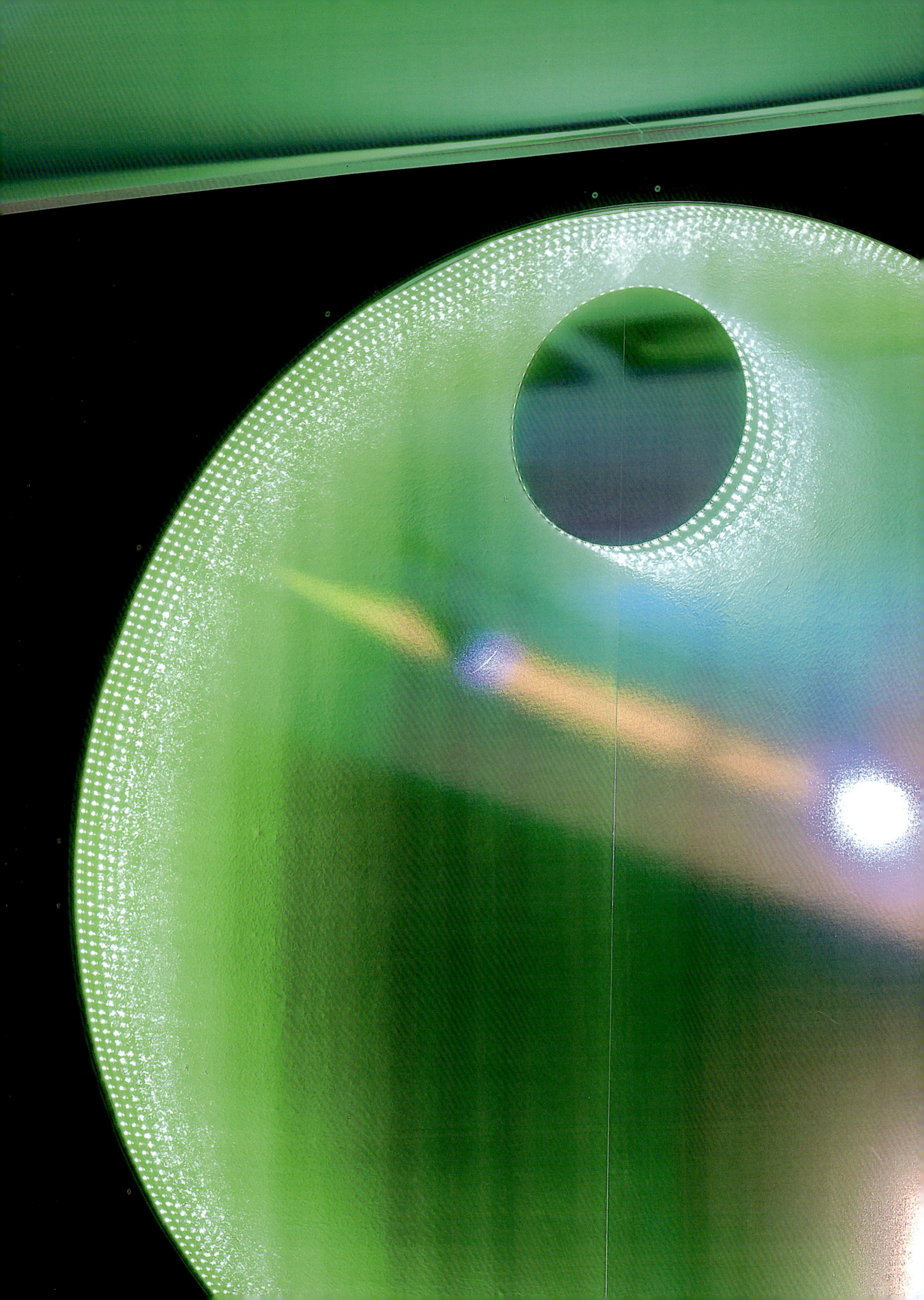

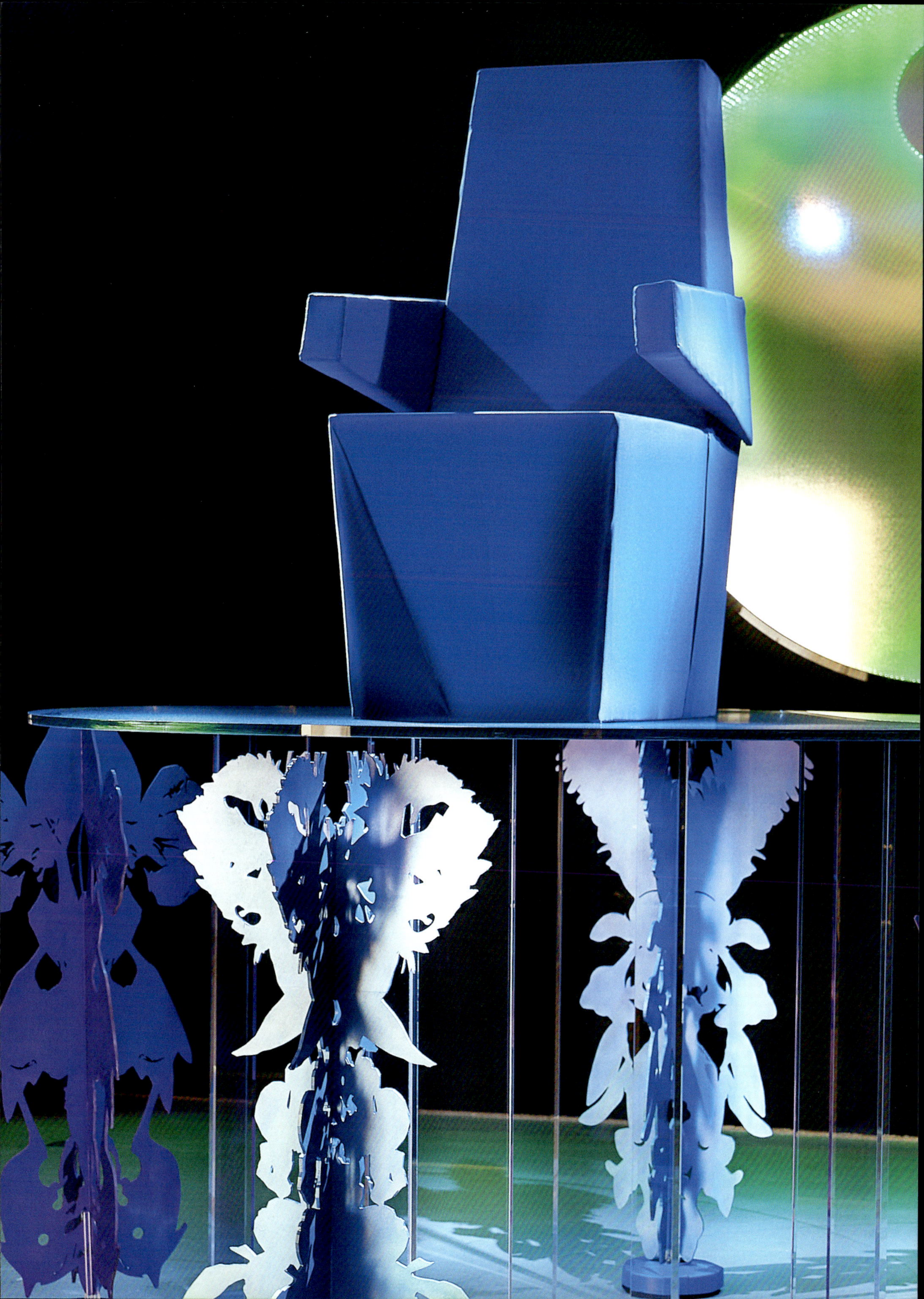

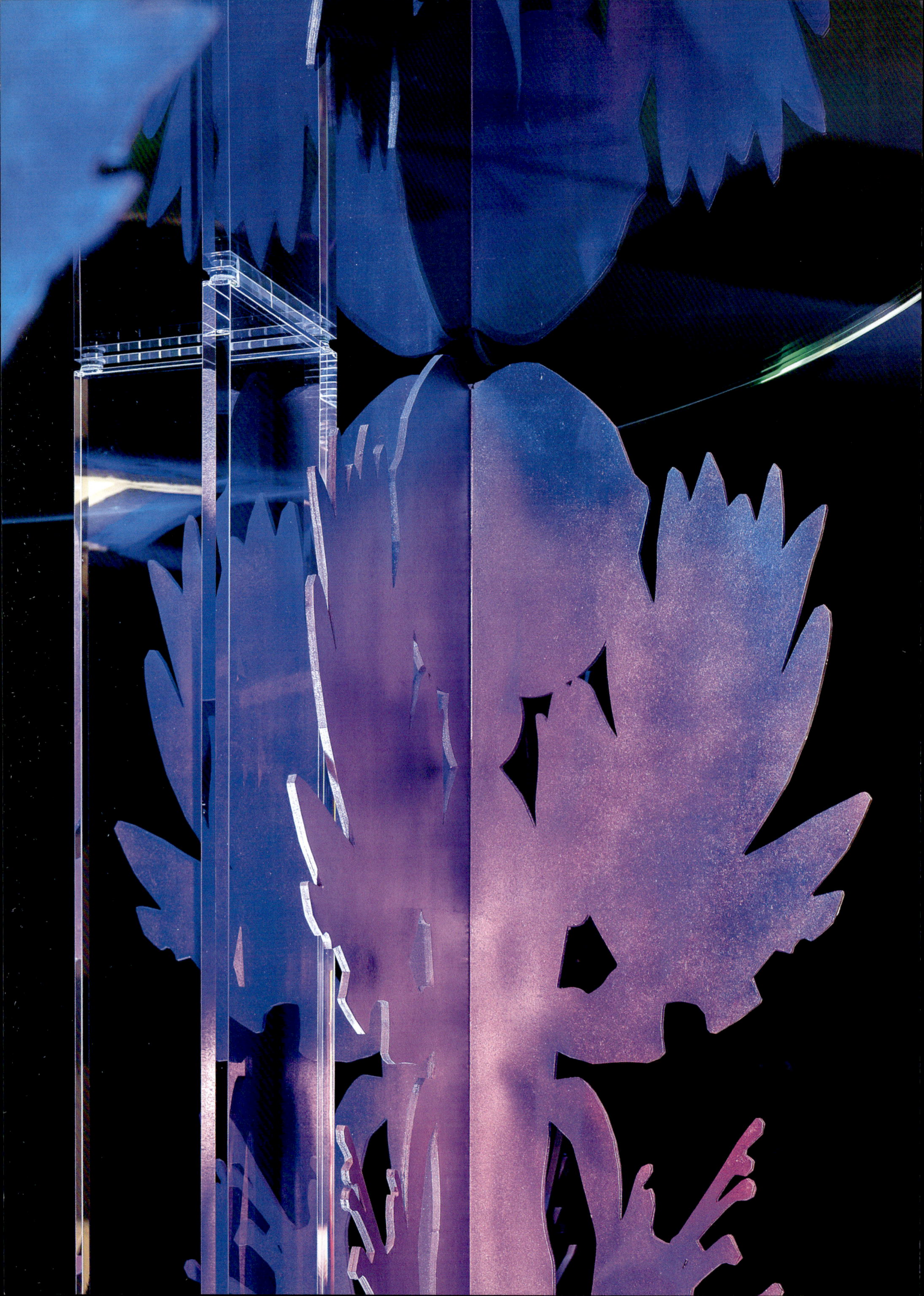

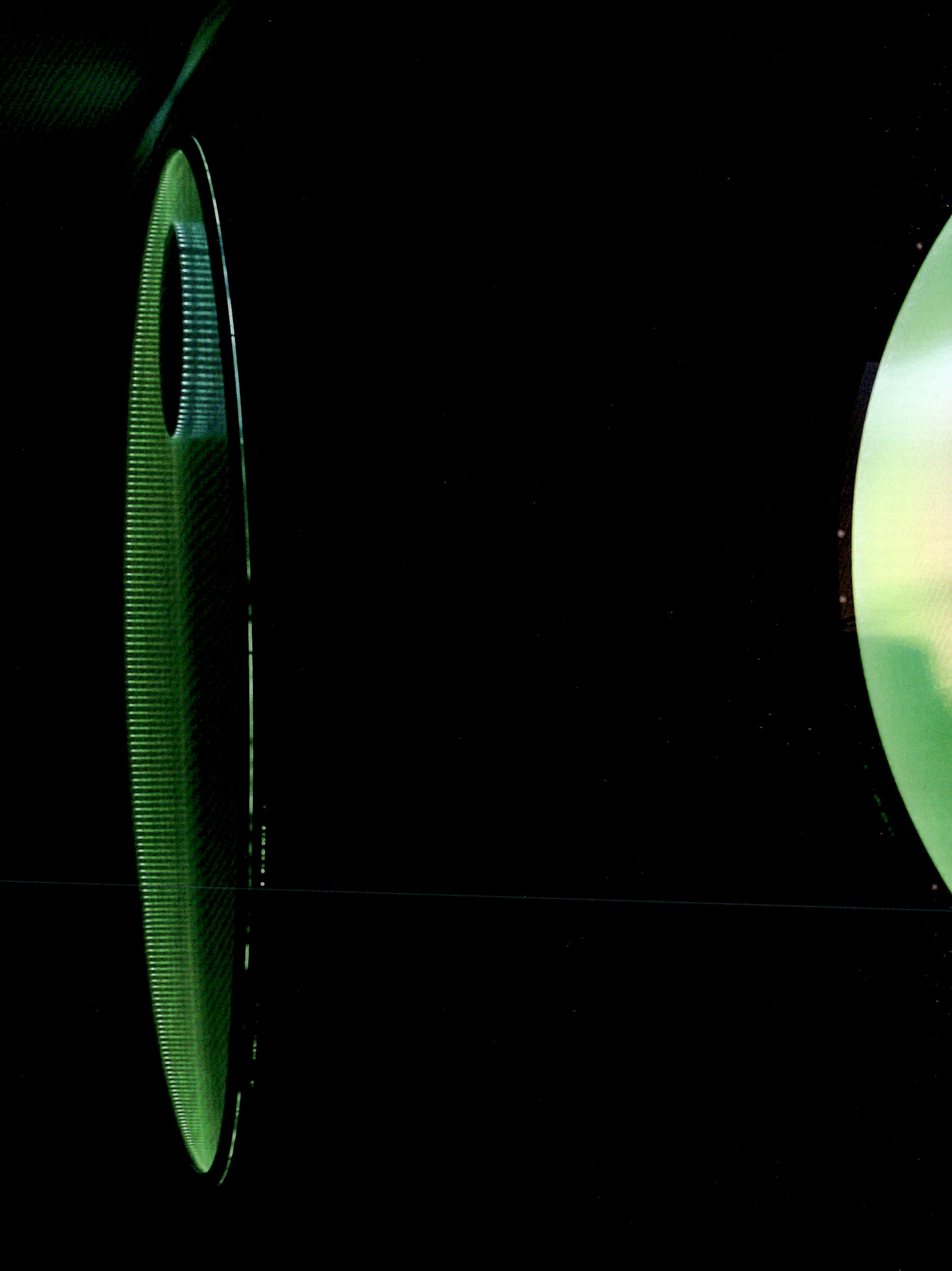

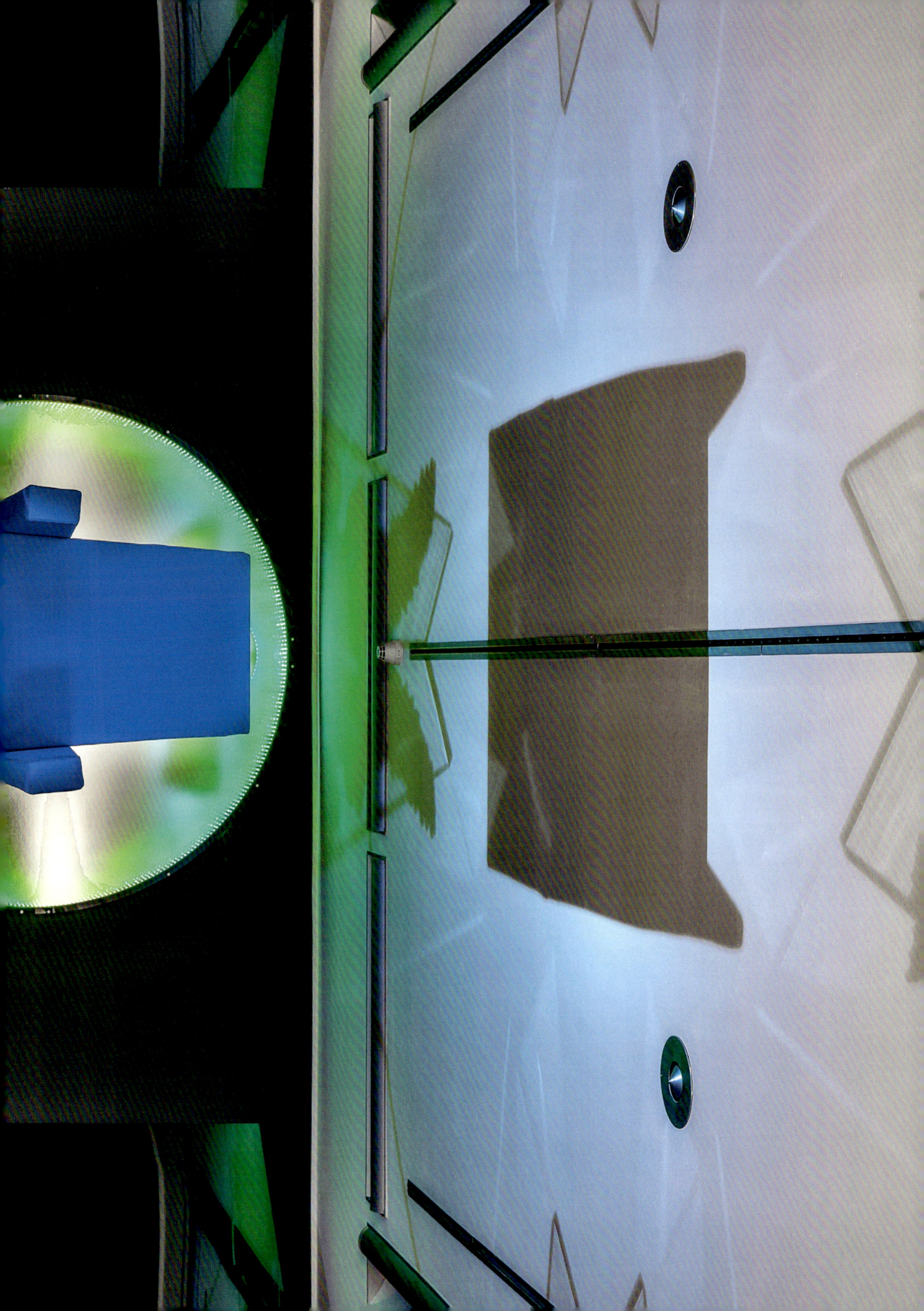

I zoom out, zoom in, into structures—for
instance by taking one element such as
a window that embodies or represents the
bigger picture, like a fractal.

I wanted to tell the story of the group
of people that are not usually the main
protagonists or even mentioned. The
ones that are always kind of on the
periphery. Even if you see images of them
here and there on the news, they won't
pass the screen and remain trapped
on that surface. So, they're always
stuck on the border. This is something
similar to windows, as the view one sees
is a fragment of a bigger thing, again
predefined by the architect. If something
is directly on the window pane, it's never
in or out.

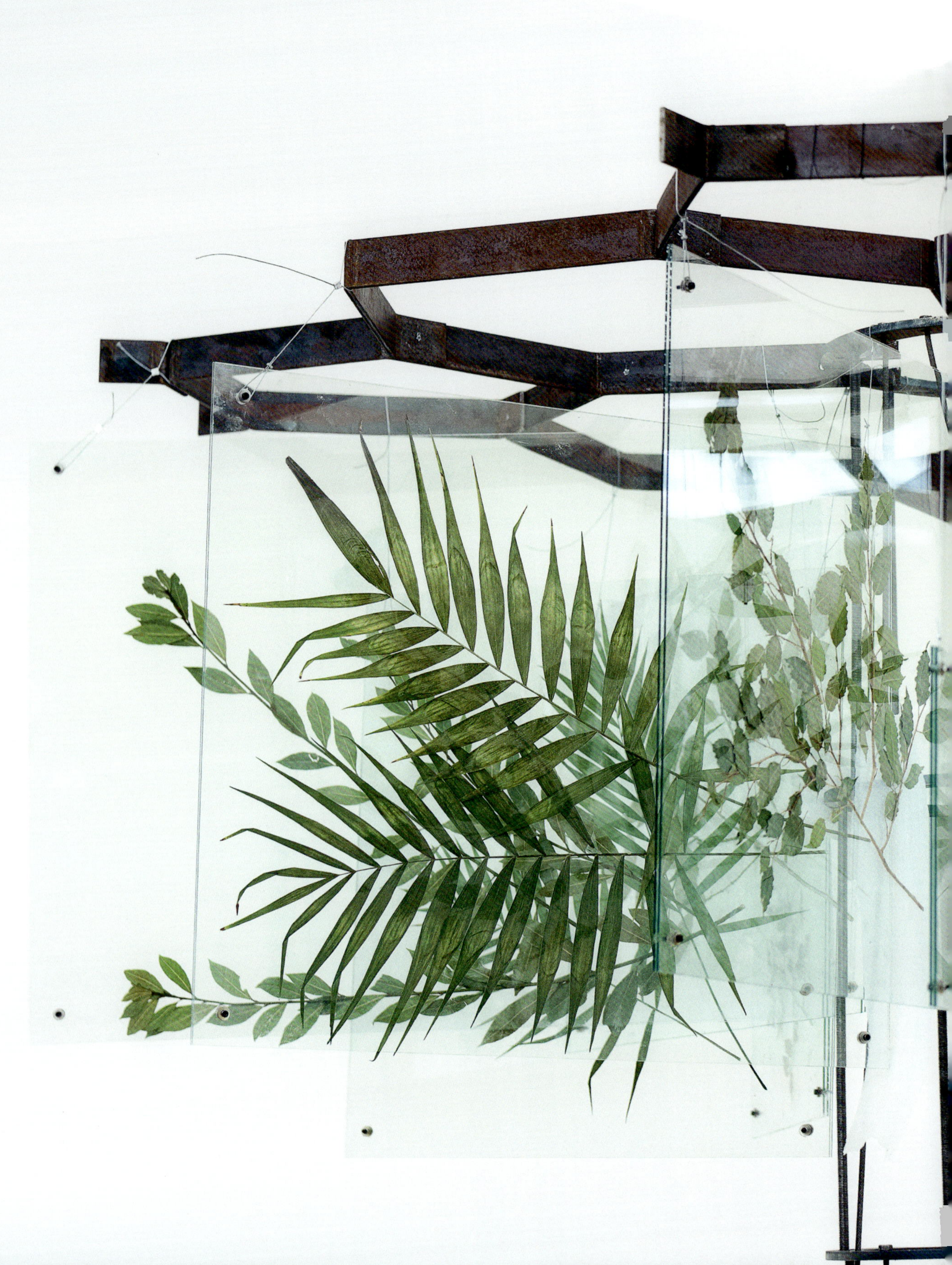

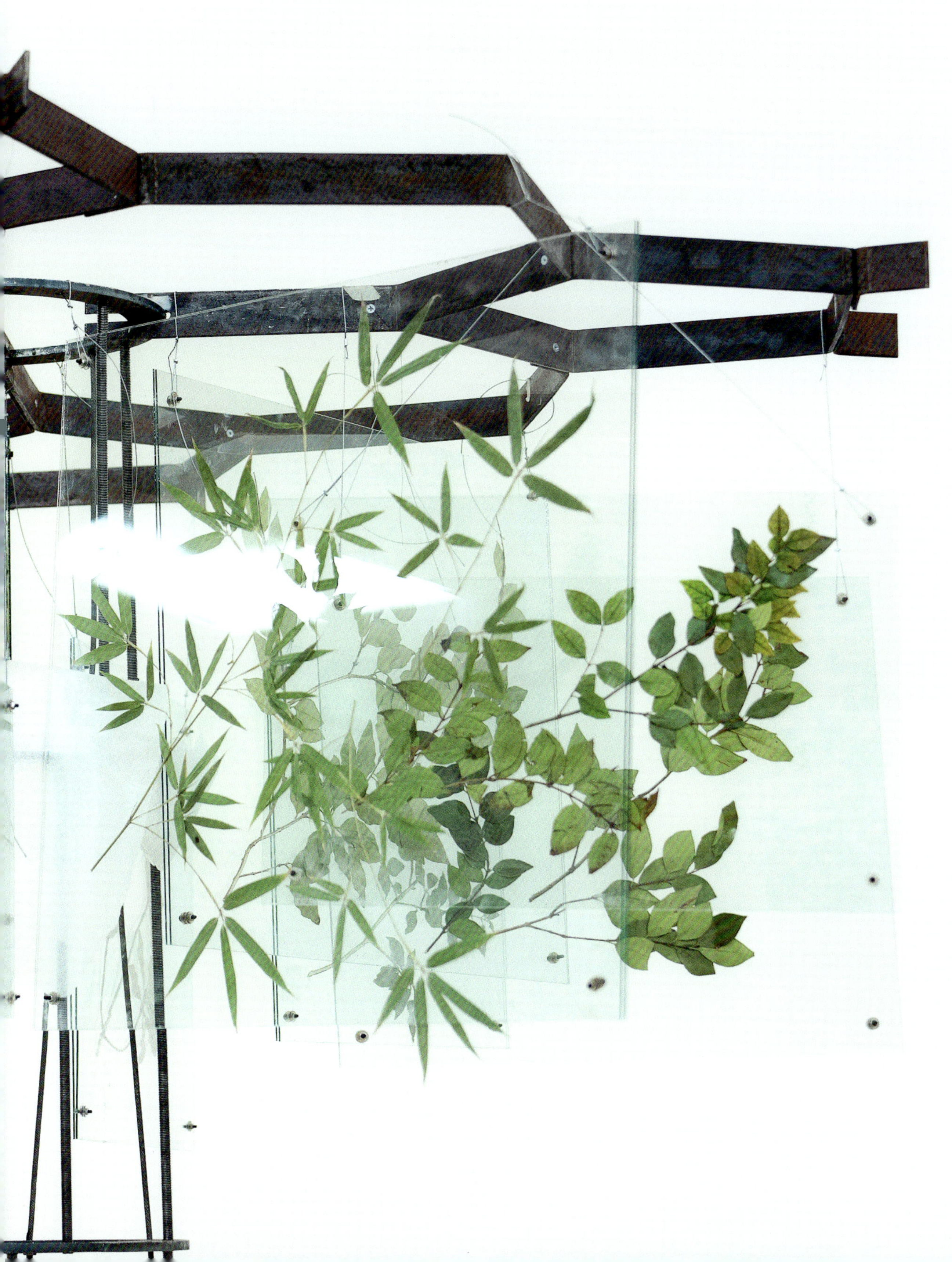

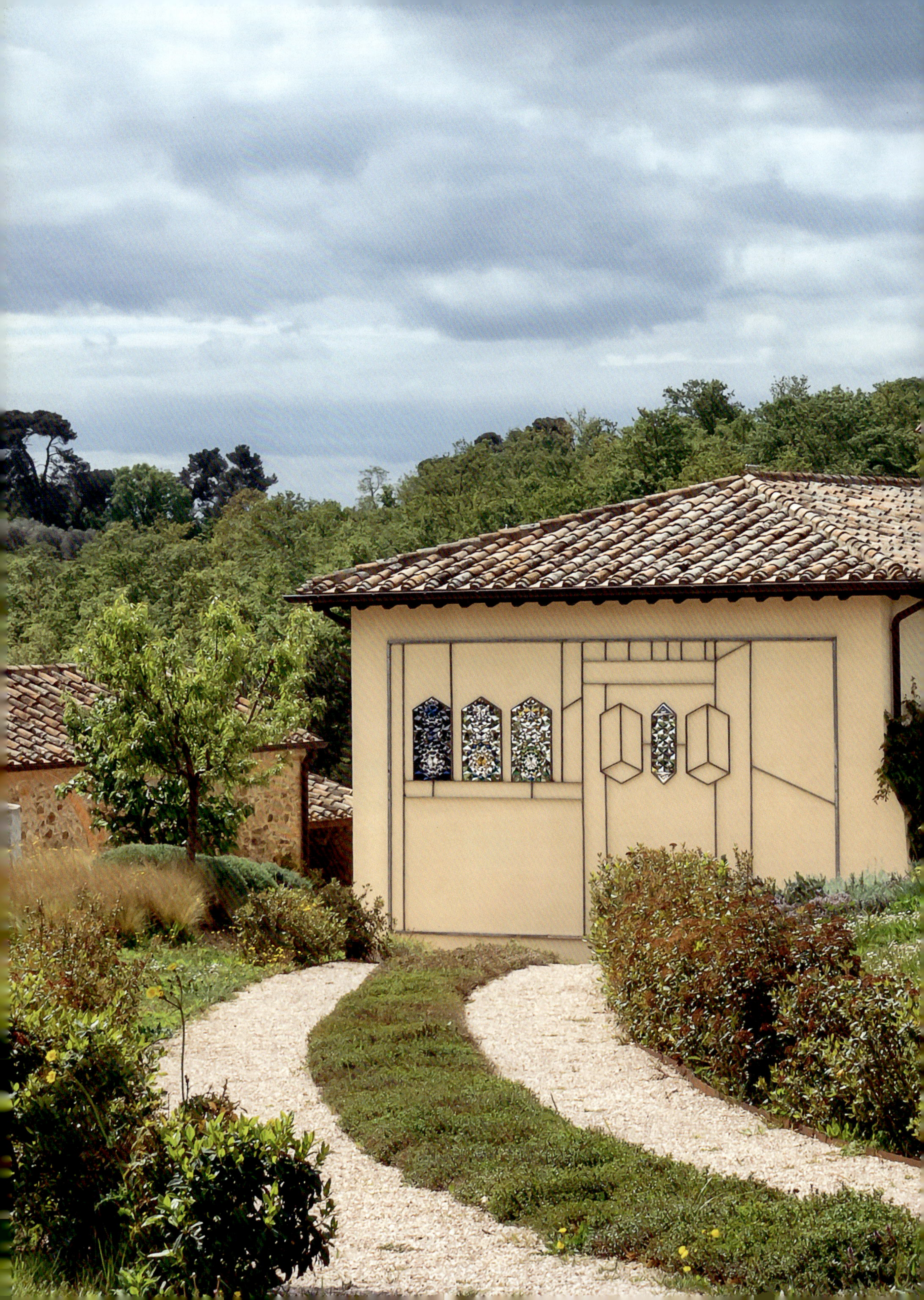

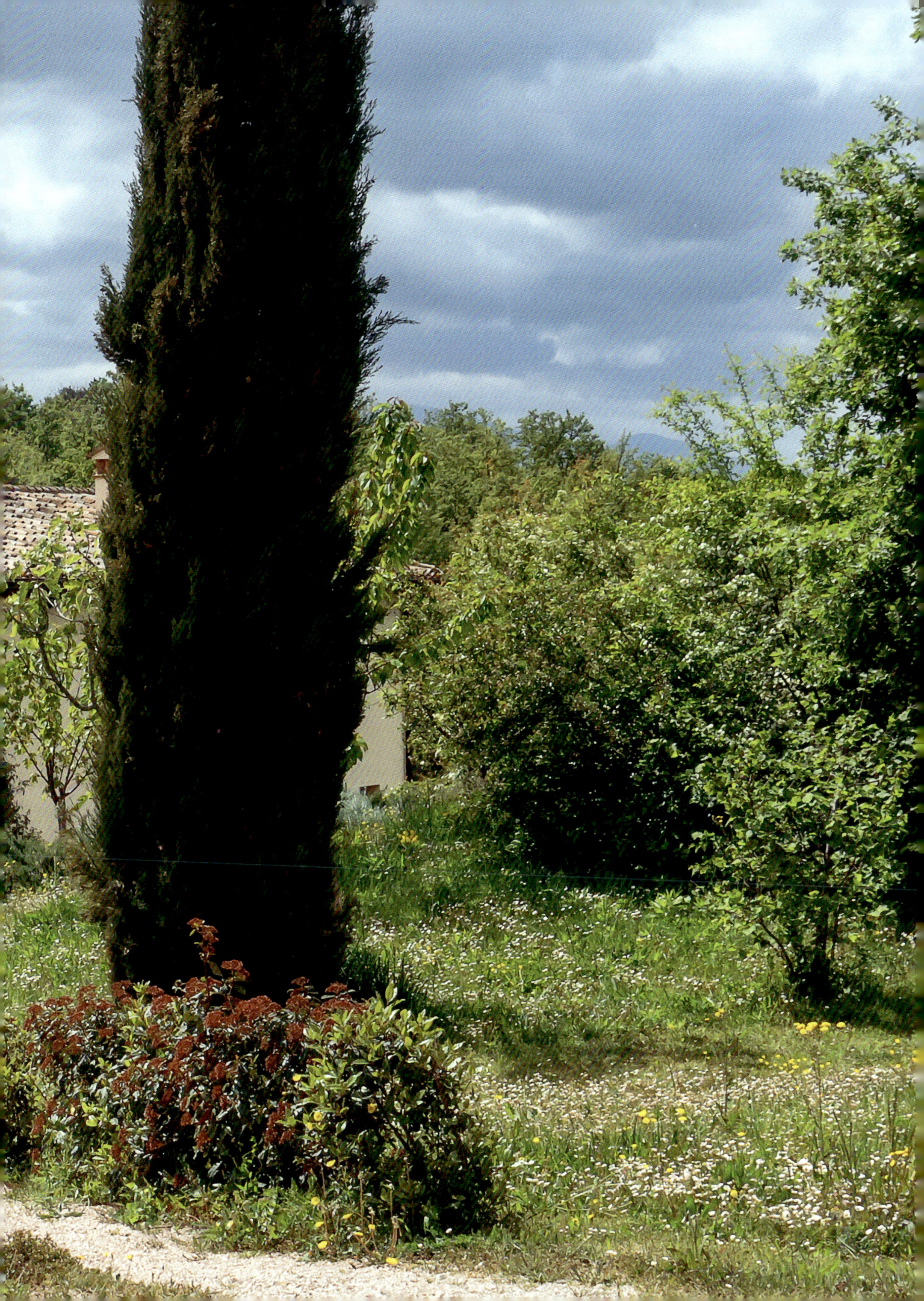

Neda Saeedi; Whispers is part of the Podere Trafonti Notebooks series following the artist's residency at Podere Trafonti (www.poderetrafonti.com) during the summer of 2023.

The book was published on the occasion of the exhibition *NEDA SAEEDI; in fire yet we trust* (14 September–17 November 2024) at Taxispalais Kunsthalle Tirol.

Led by Antonella Notari Vischer and Bernard Vischer, the Trafonti Art Residency welcomes an artist per year for two months and offers emerging to mid-career artists time and space to reflect on their work and deepen their practice. The residency is intended for visual artists who work with a variety of media including sculpture, digital technologies, sound, music, film, photography, painting, performance and writing.

The artist is selected in conversation with a jury of three renowned art advisers composed for the 2023 selection by Lucia Pietroiousti (independent curator, founder of the General Ecology project at Serpentine, London), Yann Chateigné Tytelman (independent curator, editor and writer, Brussels) and Yasmin Afschar (curator, Interim Director Kunsthalle Mainz, Zurich and Mainz).

The texts in this book are also available in Italian, accessible through the following QR code.

Publisher
Mousse Publishing, Milan

Managing Editor
Bernard Vischer

Publishing Editor
Ilaria Bombelli

Publishing Concept
Yasmin Afschar and Neda Saeedi

Texts
Yasmin Afschar and Carina Bukuts

The interspersed quotes are taken from a conversation between Ana Teixeira Pinto and Neda Saeedi, published in: *Neda Saeedi, Only Birds Who Fly the Highest Can Shatter the Windows* (Florence: Villa Romana, 2022).

Translations
Gioia Guerzoni

Proofreading
Bennett Bazalgette-Staples, George MacBeth

Graphic Design
Maximage

Images
All artworks and process images are courtesy of © Neda Saeedi

Printing
Grafiche Veneziane, Venice, Italy

First edition: 2024

Image credits
Sinking Suns, 2024. Multimedia installation, glass assemblage, altered overhead projectors, digital photography. Photo © Studio Neda Saeedi (pp. 5–6, 31–39)
Whispers Across Horizons, 2024. Mirror wall sculptures, stainless steel structure, Podere Trafonti. Photo © Andrea Della Giovampaola (pp. 67, 91–96, 120–121)
In the Depth of the Night, Sky Sees the Sun, 2023. Stained glass, stainless steel structure, League Square, Prizren. Photo © Tuğhan Anıt, Autostrada Biennale (pp. 49–54, 70)
Sunsets Are Not Overrated, 2022. In collaboration with Setareh Shahbazi, projection-performance, two-channel video projection, two overhead projectors, various found objects and glass, sound, ca. 25 min. On the occasion of lumbung Film–AFTER CINEMA at documenta fifteen, Gloria Kino Kassel. Photo © Documenta 15 (pp. 40–46, 71)
Only Birds Who Fly the Highest Can Shatter the Windows, 2022. Stained glass, stainless steel structure. Photo © Studio Neda Saeedi (pp. 6–7, 55–64, 74)
Eziekel Dreams Beyond Repair, 2021. Multimedia installation, Taxispalais Kunsthalle Tirol, Innsbruck. Photo © Günter Kresser (pp. 10, 75, 109–114)
Two Shades of Green, 2021. Multimedia installation, Staatliche Kunsthalle Baden-Baden. Photo © Eunice Maurice/Argo Factory, Pejman Foundation, Tehran. Photo © Atoosa Alebooye (pp. 78, 81–90, 118–119)
Garden of Eden Moving; A Petrified Tribe, 2018/2019. Multimedia installation. Luleå Biennial 2018, Sweden. Photo © Luleå Biennial 2018/Dastan Basement Gallery, Tehran. Photo © Matin Jameie (pp. 8–9, 79, 99–108).

Acknowledgements
Neda Saeedi would like to thank Ana Teixeira Pinto, Andres Villarreal, Antonella Notari Vischer, Azin Feizabadi, Bernard Vischer, Carina Bukuts, Nina Tabassomi, Sina Ahmadi and Yasmin Afschar

Special thanks are due to:
The Shadow Foundation, Rolle (CH)
Taxispalais Kunsthalle Tirol

Published and distributed by
Mousse Publishing
Contrappunto s.r.l.
Via Pier Candido Decembrio 28
20137, Milan–Italy

Available through
Mousse Publishing, Milan
moussemagazine.it

DAP|Distributed Art Publishers, New York
artbook.com

Les presses du réel, Dijon
lespressesdureel.com

Antenne Books, London
antennebooks.com

Idea books, Amsterdam
ideabooks.nl

LibroCo, Firenze
libroco.it

ISBN 978-88-6749-658-7

€ 27 / $ 30